Seal of the State of Louisiana

CHRONOLOGY AND DOCUMENTARY
HANDBOOK OF THE
STATE OF
LOUISIANA

ROBERT I. VEXLER

State Editor

WILLIAM F. SWINDLER

Series Editor

1978 OCEANA PUBLICATIONS, INC./Dobbs Ferry, New York

Library of Congress Cataloging in Publication Data

Main entry under title:

Chronology and documentary handbook of the State of
Louisiana.

   (Chronologies and documentary handbooks of the States;
v. 18)
   Bibliography: p.
   Includes index.
   SUMMARY: Contains a chronology of historical events
from 1519 to 1977, a biographical directory of prominent citizens,
and copies of pertinent documents.
   1. Louisiana — History — Chronology. 2. Louisiana —
Biography. 3. Louisiana — History — Sources. [1. Louisiana
— History] I. Vexler, Robert I. II. Series.
F369.C47   976.3   78-6086
ISBN 0-379-16143-5

Manufactured in the United States of America

TABLE OF CONTENTS

ACKNOWLEDGMENT

Special recognition should be accorded Melvin Hecker, whose research has made a valuable contribution to this volume.

Thanks to my wife, Francine, in appreciation of her help in the preparation of this work.

Thanks also to my children, David and Melissa, without whose patience and understanding I would have been unable to devote the considerable time necessary for completing the state chronology series.

Robert I. Vexler

ACKNOWLEDGEMENTS

INTRODUCTION

This projected series of <u>Chronologies and Documentary Handbooks of the States</u> will ultimately comprise fifty separate volumes - one for each of the states of the Union. Each volume is intended to provide a concise ready reference of basic data on the state, and to serve as a starting point for more extended study as the individual user may require. Hopefully, it will be a guidebook for a better informed citizenry - students, civic and service organizations, professional and business personnel, and others.

The editorial plan for the <u>Handbook</u> series falls into six divisions: (1) a chronology of selected events in the history of the state; (2) a short biographical directory of the principal public officials, e.g., governors, Senators and Representatives; (3) a short biographical directory of prominent personalities of the state (for most states); (4) the first state constitution; (5) the text of some representative documents illustrating main currents in the political, economic, social or cultural history of the state; and (6) a selected bibliography for those seeking further or more detailed information. Most of the data found in the present volume, in fact, have been taken from one or another of these references.

The current constitutions of all fifty states, as well as the federal Constitution, are regularly kept up to date in the definitive collection maintained by the Legislative Drafting Research Fund of Columbia University and published by the publisher of the present series of <u>Handbooks</u>. These texts are available in most major libraries under the title, <u>Constitutions of the United States: National and State</u>, in two volumes, with a companion volume, the <u>Index Digest of State Constitutions</u>.

Finally, the complete collection of documents illustrative of the constitutional development of each state, from colonial or territorial status up to the current constitution as found in the Columbia University collection, is being prepared for publication in a multi-volume series by the present series editor. Whereas the present series of <u>Handbooks</u> is intended for a wide range of interested citizens, the series of annotated constitutional materials in the volumes of <u>Sources and Documents of U. S. Constitutions</u> is primarily for the specialist in government, history or law. This is not to suggest that the general citizenry may not profit equally from referring to these materials; rather, it points up the separate purpose of the <u>Handbooks</u>, which is to guide the user to these and other sources of authoritative information with which he may systematically enrich his knowledge of this state and its place in the American Union.

William F. Swindler
Series Editor

Robert I. Vexler
Series Associate Editor

Union, Justice and Confidence

State Motto

CHRONOLOGY

1519 Alonso Alvarez de Piñeda discovered the possible mouth of the Mississippi.

1541 Hernando de Soto explored part of the region of what is now Louisiana and discovered the Mississippi River for Spain.

1542 Survivors of Hernando de Soto's expedition traveled down the Mississippi River to its mouth.

1682 April 9. Robert Cavalier, Sieur de La Salle helped to establish Louisiana.

1683 Father Hennepin published his work Description de la Louisiane.

1684 Robert Cavalier, Sieur de La Salle began his two-year effort to discover the mouth of the Mississippi.

Henri de Tonty travelled down the Mississippi River in a vain attempt to meet Robert de La Salle.

April 14. Louis XIV issued a patent which named Robert de La Salle governor of Louisiana.

1686 April 9. Henri de Tonty and thirty Frenchmen along with five Indians reached the Gulf of Mexico. When Tonty left to travel up the Mississippi again, he proceeded to negotiate aliances with the tribes along the river.

1699 February 9. Pierre le Moyne, Sieur d'Iberville discovered a channel with 24 feet of water between his ship and the Cat Islands in a search for a channel which would lead to a safe harbor.

February 27. The search for the Mississippi from the Gulf of Mexico began.

March 2. Pierre le Moyne, Sieur d'Iberville, discovered the mouth of the Mississippi.

April 8. Construction of Fort Maurepas on the Bay of Biloxi began.

A. le Moyne, Sieur de Sauvolle, became the French governor of Louisiana. He died in office in 1701.

1700   March 22 or 23. The Spanish Governor of Pensecola, Arriola, arrived with three ships and some 200 men to visit Fort Maurepas and indicate Spanish displeasure.

1701   Jean Baptiste Le Moyne, Sieur de Bienville, became the French governor of Louisiana and served until 1713.

1702   January 12. Jean Baptiste Le Moyne, Sieur de Bienville, and Joseph Le Moyne, Sieur de Sérigny, travelled to Mobile Bay with instructions to construct a fort, which was called Fort St. Louis.

March 3. Iberville arrived at Fort St. Louis to supervise construction.

March 25. Henri de Tonty appeared at Fort St. Louis with some Indian chiefs.

March 31. Pierre Le Moyne, Sieur d'Iberville, sailed for France.

1704   July. **Twenty-seven marriageable females arrived at Mobile from France.**

Nicholas de La Salle made a census of the area. There were 180 men bearing arms, 27 French families with 10 children, 6 Indian boys and 5 Indian slave girls, and 4 priests.

1708   Nicholas de La Salle's census showed that there were 279 persons.

1710   May 10. Antoine de La Mothe Cadillac was named governor of Louisiana. He arrived on June 5, 1713. He served until 1716.

1712   September 14. King Louis XIV granted the wealthy merchant, Antoine Crozat, exclusive rights to carry out trade in Louisiana for fifteen years.

1714   The first permanent French settlement was established at Natchitoches.

1716   The Sieur de Bienville was the acting French governor of Louisiana.

October 26. Jean Michiele, Seigneur de Lépinay and de la Longueville was appointed governor of Louisiana. He arrived May 9,

1717. After having fought with many individuals, Lépinay was recalled on September 20,
1717.

August. Antoine Crozat gave up his ruinous
commercial monopoly in Louisiana.

September 6. John Law's company, the Company
of the West, was chartered for a twenty-five
year period, granting it a complete monopoly
of trade in Louisiana. The company merged
with the Company of East India and the Company of China. The company first tried to
send voluntary colonists and then convicts.
The agents went to various parts of Europe to
recruit colonists, especially among the Ger-
mans.

1718   March 15 - April 15. Sometime during this
            period work was begun on the town of New Or-
            leans. It was founded by the Governor Jean
            Baptiste le Moyne, Sieur de Bienville. He
            had been appointed in 1718 and served in of-
            fice until 1724.

1720   December 20. John Law fled France when his
            fiscal empire was destroyed.

1721   25 prostitutes collected from a house of
            correction were sent to Louisiana in order
            to help relieve the extreme shortage of women
            and also to help in getting the Canadian set-
            tlers to leave their Indian mistresses.

1721   March. Adrien de Pauger was sent to trace
            out the plan of New Orleans.

            March. Population: New Orleans, 470; sur-
            rounding territory, 1,269.

            March. The first group of German immigrants,
            200 in number, arrived in Louisiana to settle
            near New Orleans.

1722   September 11. The first recorded tropical
            hurricane destroyed New Orleans.

            New Orleans became the seat of government.

1724   February 16. The regent, in the name of Louis
            XV ordered the Sieur de Bienville to hand over
            command of Louisiana to Le Blonde de La Tour
            and then to return to France. Bienville was

eventually granted a pension of 3,000 livres.

March. The Code Noir, Black Code, was issued
in order to protect slaves from injustice and
cruelty. It was the first such code to regulate the conduct of the Blacks.

Boisbriant served as ad interim governor of
the territory.

1726   Etienne de Périer became governor of Louisiana territory and served until 1733.

1727   August 6. Six Ursuline nuns arrived at New
Orleans to tend hospital and create a school
for girls.

1729   November 29. The Natchez Indians got into the
fort at Natchez by persuading the settlers of
their friendly intentions and then attacked
the settlers and the soldiers.

1730   January 27. Jean Paul Le Sueur led 500 Choc-
taw Indians against the Natchez Indians.

1731   January 22. King Louis XV made arrangements
to purchase the colony from the Company of
the Indies.

1732   January. The Western Company of John Law
surrendered the grant of a monopoly in Louisiana to the crown.

Louis XV appointed the Sieur de Bienville
governor of Louisiana. He served in the office until 1743.

1733   February. Bienville arrived in New Orleans.

1736   Governor Bienville led a force of approximate-
ly 1,200, half of which were Choctaws,
against the Chickasaw Indians.

1740   Cultivation of cotton began.

Winter. Governor Bienville led another expedition against the Chickasaws.

1743   May 10. The Marquis de Vaudreuil, who had
been appointed governor of Louisiana, arrived
in New Orleans. He served in office until
1753.

1751   Sugar cane was introduced into Louisiana from

Santo Domingo by the Jesuits.

1753   February 3. Louis Billouart de Kerlérec
        arrived in New Orleans as the new governor of
        Louisiana territory. He succeeded the Marquis
        de Vaudreuil who became governor of Canada
        on January 1, 1755.

1763   June 29. Jean Jacques Blaise d'Abbadie
        succeeded Louis de Kerlérec as governor of
        the territory. D'Abbadie served in office
        until his death of February 4, 1765.

        The first Acadians reached Louisiana.

1765   February 4. Captain Charles Philippe Aubry
        became governor of the territory after the
        death of Jean d'Abbadie.

1766   March 5. Don Antonio de Ullola was named the
        first Spanish governor of the territory by
        Charles III, King of Spain. De Ulloa served
        until 1768.

1768   The Créoles, supported by the Acadians and the
        Germans in Louisiana started the first revo-
        lution in America against a European monarch.
        They indicated their desire to be French ra-
        ther than Spanish subjects.

        October 27. The rebels attacked New Orleans
        and forced Governor Ullola to leave.

1769   August 18. Alexander O'Reilly, an Irishman
        and a Spanish general, landed at New Orleans
        with 3,600 troops. He arrested twelve of the
        rebels, tried them, sentencing some to death
        and other to life imprisonment.

        August 18. Louisiana was formally handed over
        to Spain.

1770   Luis de Unzaga became governor of Louisiana
        territory and served until 1777.

1777   Bernardo de Gálvez became the Spanish gover-
        nor of the territory and served until 1785.

1779   Governor Gálvez captured Munchac, Baton Rouge
        and Natchez from British forces.

1780   Governor Gálvez captured Mobile from the
        British.

1785   Estevan Miró became the Spanish governor of
              Louisiana territory and served in that capa-
              city until 1791.

1787   James Wilkinson arrived at New Orleans
              with a proposal to separate Kentucky from
              the United States and to promote trade between
              Kentucky and New Orleans. He was soon arrest-
              ed.

1788   March 21. Over 800 buildings were destroyed
              by a great fire in New Orleans.

1791   Francois Louis Hector, Baron de Carondolet
              became governor of Louisiana and served until
              December 30, 1797.

1792   October 4. The first theater opened on
              St. Peter Street in New Orleans.

1794   Governor Carondolet began publication of
              Louisiana's first newspaper, Moniteur de la
              Louisiane.

              Spain and the United States signed a treaty
              recognizing the Mississippi River as the
              boundary between the United States and Louisi-
              ana, and giving Americans the right of deposit.

1795   July. Bishop Luis Peñalver y Gárdenas, the
              first bishop of Louisiana, arrived in New
              Orleans.

              August 5. Brigadier General Manuel Gayoso
              de Lemos became governor of Louisiana, suc-
              ceeding Baron de Carondolet, who was appointed
              president of the Royal Audience of Quito.
              Governor Gayoso died on July 18. 1799.

1799   Francisco Bouligny and Nicolás María Vida
              shared a brief rule as governors of Louisiana.

              The Marquis of Caso Calva became military
              governor of Louisiana, succeeding Francisco
              Bouligny. Nicolás Vidal remained the civil
              governor. Calva served until 1801.

1800   France regained Louisiana from Spain.

1801   Brigadier General Juan Manuel de Salcedo
              became governor of Louisiana territory and
              served until 1803.

1802   October 16. Juan Ventura Morales, acting
              intendant, canceled the right of deposit at
              New Orleans which had been held by the Ameri-
              cans since 1795.

1803   March 26. Pierre Clément de Laussat, who had
              been appointed colonial prefect by Napoleon,
              arrived at New Orleans.

1803   April 30. The United States and France con-
              cluded a treaty whereby France ceded Louisi-
              ana to the United States. The treaty was
              signed May 2.

              November 30. Spain's flag was lowered after
              which the tricolor of France was raised over
              New Orleans.

              December 20. Pierre de Laussat, French col-
              onial prefect, turned Louisiana over to the
              American commissioners.

1804   March 25. Congress passed an act organizing
              the portion of Louisiana south of 33 degrees
              as the Territory of Orleans.

              October 2. William C. C. Claiborne became
              governor of the Territory of Orleans. He
              served in office until 1812.

1805   March. Congress granted the Territory of
              Orleans representative government.

              April 10. The following counties were estab-
              lished: Acadia, Concordia, Iberville, La
              Fourche, Natchitoches, Orleans, Ouachita,
              Pointe Coupee, and Rapides. Acadia, with
              its county seat at Crowley, was the original
              name of Nova Scotia, a province of Canada.
              Concordia has its seat at Vidalia. Iberville,
              with its county seat at Plaquemine, was named
              for Pierre le Moyne Iberville, who served in
              the French navy and built Fort Biloxi at Bil-
              oxi Bay. Lafourche has its county seat at
              Thibodaux. Natchitoches, with its seat at
              Natchitoches, was named for the Natchitoches
              Indian tribe. Orleans, organized March 31,
              with its seat at New Orleans, was named for
              Orleans, France. Ouachita, with its seat at
              Monroe, was organized March 31, 1807, and
              named for the Ouachita Indian tribe. Pointe
              Coupee has its seat at New Roads. Rapides
              has its county seat at Alexandria.

June 26. Aaron Burr reached New Orleans after having killed Alexander Hamilton in a duel and having resigned from the office of Vice President of the United States. He was entertained by Edward Livingston and Daniel Clark. Burr was soon accused of plotting to separate the western states and territories from the United States with the intention of establishing a new nation. He was eventually captured in Mississippi.

1807   March 31. The following counties were created: Ascension, Assumption, Avoyelles, Plaquemines, St. Bernard, St. Charles, St. James, St. John the Baptist, St. Landry, St. Martin, and West Baton Rouge. Ascension, with its seat at Donaldson, was named for the Ascension of Jesus. Assumption has its county seat at Napoleonville. Avoyelles, with Marksville as its county seat, was named for the Avoyelles Indian tribe. Plaquemines has its county seat at Pointe-a-la-Hache. St. Bernard, with its seat at Chalmette, was named for St. Bernard of Clairvaux. St. Charles, with its seat at Hahnville, was named for Saint Charles Borromeo, an archbishop and cardinal. St. James has its seat at Convent. St. John the Baptist County has its seat at Edgard. St. Landry, with its seat at Upelousas, was named for Saint Landri, Bishop of Paris. St. Martin County, with St. Martinville as its seat, was named for Saint Martin, who became Bishop of Tours. West Baton Rouge County has its seat at Port Allen.

1808   March 23. Catahoula County was established, with its seat at Harrisonburg. It was named for the Catahoula Indian tribe.

1810   Population: 76,556.

September 26. The West Floridians, having risen in rebellion, seized Baton Rouge and proclaimed their independence.

October 27. St. Helena and St. Tammany Counties were established. St. Helena, with Greensburg as its county seat, was named for Saint Helen, the mother of Constantine the Great. St. Tammany, with its seat at Covington, was named for Tammany, chief of the Delaware Indians.

October 27. The United States annexed the
area known as the West Feliciana District
around Baton Rouge from Spain after the
Americans had captured the area.

East Baton Rouge County was established, with
Baton Rouge as its seat.

The territorial legislature authorized a
lottery to raise $10,000 for the first Epis-
copal church in Louisiana, Christ Church.

1811   January 14. The United States Congress passed
            a bill authorizing the Territory of Orleans
            to organize itself as a state.

            April 17. St. Mary County, with its seat at
            Franklin, was created. It was named for
            Mary, the mother of Jesus.

            November. A constitutional convention met
            at New Orleans and wrote a constitution.

            A slave insurrection occurred in St. John the
            Baptist Parish, or County, forty miles north
            of New Orleans.

1812   January 10. The first steamboat arrived at
            New Orleans, the New Orleans.

            April 30. Louisiana was admitted to the Union
            as the 18th state.

            William C. C. Claiborne, Democrat-Republican,
            became governor of the state. He served in
            office until 1812.

1814   December. Captain Henry Miller Shreeve came
            down the Mississippi to New Orleans.

            December 2. General Andrew Jackson and his
            forces reached New Orleans.

            December 14. The Battle of New Orleans opened
            on Lake Borgne, east of New Orleans. It
            finally ended on January 19, 1815 at Fort St.
            Philip on the Mississippi River, with a vic-
            tory for General Jackson and his troops.

1815   January 8. The actual Battle of New Orleans
            was fought with a victory for the American
            forces under General Jackson. Jackson Day
            was made a legal holiday.

1816   Jacques Villeré, Democrat-Republican, became
                governor of the state and served until
                1820

1819   March 6. Washington County was established,
                with its seat at Franklinton, and was named
                for George Washington, commander of the Con-
                tinental Army and first President of the
                United States.

1820   Population: 153,407.

                Thomas B. Robertson, Democrat-Republican,
                became governor of Louisiana and served until
                his resignation in 1822.

1822   March 22. Terrebonne County, with its
                county seat at Houma, was established.

                The state legislature passed an act permitting
                a lottery to raise $30,000 for a Presbyterian
                Church at New Orleans.

                Henry S. Thibodaux, Democrat-Republican, be-
                came governor of the state as a result of
                the resignation of Governor Thomas B. Robert-
                son. Thibodaux served in the office until
                1824.

1823   January 17. Lafayette County was created,
                with its seat at Mayo. It was named for the
                Marquis de Lafayette, who resigned from the
                French army to aid the Americans in the Revo-
                lutionary War. He was commissioned a major
                general in the Continental Army.

1824   February 17. East Feliciana and West Feli-
                ciana Counties were established. East Feli-
                ciana has its seat at Clinton, and West Fe-
                liciana at St. Francisville.

                Henry S. Johnson, Demcrat-Republican, became
                governor of the state. He served in the gu-
                bernatorial office until 1828.

1825   February 11. Jefferson County was created,
                with its seat at Gretna. It was named for
                Thomas Jefferson, writer and signer of the
                Declaration of Independence, Secretary of
                State in the Cabinet of President George
                Washington, Vice President of the United
                States under President John Adams, and third
                President of the United States.

Donaldson was the nominal capital of the
state until 1831.

Centenary College of Louisiana was founded
at Shreveport.

1826   The state legislature passed a bill authoriz-
ing a lottery to raise $20,000 for the Catho-
lic Church of St. Francis.

1827   A group of French-American students organized
a procession of street maskers on Shrove Tues-
day. They began the first Mardi Gras cele-
bration in New Orleans.

1828   March 13. Claiborne County was created, with
its county seat at Homer. It was named for
William Charles Coles Claiborne, first governor of Louisiana Territory and the first
governor of the state of Louisiana.

Pierre Derbigny, National Republican, became
governor of the state. He served in the office until his death on October 1, 1829.

1829   October 1. Armand Beauvais, president of the
State Senate, became governor upon the death
of Pierre Derbigny. Beauvais served in the
office until 1830.

1830   Population: 215,739.

Jacques Dupre became governor of the state
and served in office until 1831.

1831   May 24. Edward Livingston became Secretary
of State in the Cabinet of President Andrew
Jackson.

André B. Roman, National Republican, became
governor of the state. He served in the office until 1835.

1832   February 10. Livingston County was created,
with Livingston as its county seat. It was
named for Robert R. Livingston, member of the
Continental Congress, Chancellor of New York
State, who administered the oath of office
to President George Washington, April 30,
1789.

1833   The state legislature banned lotteries.

1834   Tulane University of Louisiana was founded at
            New Orleans.

1835   Edward D. White, Whig, became governor of
            the state. He served in the office until
            1839.

1838   January 18. Caddo County was created, with
            its county seat at Shreveport. It was named
            for the Caddo Indian tribe.

            March 6. Caldwell County, with its seat at
            Columbia, was established. It was named for
            Matthew Caldwell, a frontiersman from North
            Carolina.

1839   January 19. Madison County was created, with
            its seat at Tallulah. It was named for James
            Madison, Secretary of State in the Cabinet of
            President Thomas Jefferson, and fourth Presi-
            dent of the United States.

            March 13. Union County, with Farmerville as
            its seat, was established.

            André B. Roman, Whig, became governor of the
            state. He served in the gubernatorial office
            until 1843.

1840   Population: 352,411.

            March 24. Calcasieu County was created, with
            Lake Charles as its County seat.

            New Orleans became the second largest Ameri-
            can port because of the steamboat traffic on
            the Mississippi River.

1843   February 24. Bossier County was established,
            with its seat at Benton. It was named for
            Pierre Evariste John Baptiste Bossier, a Rep-
            resentative from Louisiana.

            March 1. Franklin County, with its county
            seat at Winnsboro, was created. It was named
            for Benjamin Franklin, an American official,
            member of the Continental Congress, signer of
            the Declaration of Independence, and member of
            the Constitutional Convention.

            March 7. Sabine County was established, with
            Many as its county seat.

March 17. Tensas County, with St. Joseph as
its county seat, was created. It was named
for the Tensas Indian tribe.

April 1. De Soto County was established, with
its seat at Mansfield. It was named for Hernando De Soto.

Alfred Mouton, Whig, became governor of the
state. He served in office until 1846.

1844 March 25. Morehouse County was created, with
Bostrop as its county seat. It was named
for Abraham Morehouse. Vermilion County,
with Abbeville as its seat, was also established.

March 30. Vernon County was created, with
Leesville as the county seat. It was named
for Mount Vernon, George Washington's home.

1845 February 25. Jackson County was established,
with Jonesboro as its seat. It was named for
Andrew Jackson, major-general in the United
States Army, who won a victory at New Orleans,
captured Florida, and was seventh President of
the United States.

A new state constitution was adopted which
prohibited a lottery.

1846 January. James Dunwoody DeBow began editing
the <u>Commercial Review of the South and South-
west</u> at New Orleans.

Isaac Johnson, Democrat, became governor of
Lousiana, serving until 1850.

1847 February 16. Tulane University of Lousiana
received its charter in New Orleans as the
University of Louisiana. It was partially
supported by the state, awarding its first
degrees in 1857. It changed its name in
1884.

1848 March 14. Bienville County was established,
with Arcadia as its seat. It was named for
Jean Baptiste LeMoyne, Sieur de Bienville,
the French governor of Louisiana who established New Orleans.

March 16. Red River County was created, with
its county seat at Coushatta.

1849   Baton Rouge became the capital of the state.
            It remained the capital until 1864.

1850   Population: 517,762.

            August 15. Charles M. Conrad became Secretary
            of War in the Cabinet of President Millard
            Fillmore.

            Joseph M. Walker, Democrat, became governor
            of the state. He served in office until
            1853.

1851   Phineas T. Barnum brought Jenny Lind to New
            Orleans where she sang fourteen concerts be-
            fore packed houses.

1852   February 24. Winn County was established,
            with Winnfield as its seat. It was named
            for Walter O. Winn, an attorney of Alexandria,
            Louisiana.

            March 11. Richland County, with its seat at
            Rayville, was created.

            A new constitution was adopted.

1853   March 31. Louisiana State University re-
            ceived its charter at Alexandria as the Loui-
            siana State Seminary of Learning and Military
            Academy. It offered its first degrees in
            1869 and moved to Baton Rouge in 1870, at
            which time it became Louisiana State Univer-
            sity.

            Paul O. Hébert, Democrat, became governor of
            the state. He served in office until 1856.

            A yellow fever epidemic broke out at New Or-
            leans. Approximately 5,000 persons died of
            it during the next two years.

1856   August 10. 400 people, who were attending
            a ball on Last Island died when strong winds
            drove high waves over the island.

            Robert C. Wickliffe, Democrat, became gover-
            nor of Louisiana. He served in office until
            1860.

1857   Decorated floats were first used in the New
            Orleans Mardi Gras. This aspect was insti-
            tuted by the Mystic Krewe of Comus, a secret

organization, founded in the same year.

1860   Population: 708,002

Thomas O. Moore, Democrat, became governor
of the state. He was to serve until 1864,
but only was in office until 1862 when a
military governor was appointed by the Union.

1861   January 26. A state convention adopted a
session ordinance and thus became the sixth
state to leave the union.

December 3. Union troops landed at Ship Island.

1862   April. Admiral D. G. Farragut traveled up
the Mississippi River with a strong fleet.
He went passed Forts Jackson and St. Philip,
which defended the approach to New Orleans.
General B. F. Butler occupied the city.

May 1. New Orleans surrended to the Northern
forces after the forts had been bombarded by
Admiral David G. Farragut.

May. Baton Rouge was captured.

December. The Union military government,
under George F. Shepley, the military governor, ordered elections for Congress. Those
men elected were admitted to Congress in February 1863. Governor Shepley served until
1864.

1863   July. Union forces captured Vicksburg and
Port Hudson. The entire state was now at
the mercy of the Union armies.

Fall. General Henry Watkins Allen was elected
governor of the state. He was the last elected Confederate Governor and served from 1864
to 1865.

January 8. General N. P. Banks issued a
proclamation which called for elections on
February 22 to select a governor, lieutenant
governor, secretary of state, treasurer, and
other officers.

February 22. Michael Hahn was elected governor of the state, within Union lines.

March. A state government was established
under the direction of President Abraham
Lincoln. Michael Hahn became governor and
served until March 1865.

March 28. An election was held at General
Bank's direction for delegates to a state
constitutional convention.

April. The Louisiana Constitutional Convention met. The constitution which was framed
was later adopted by the people of the state.
The convention abolished slavery.

April. Confederate troops commanded by General Richard Taylor were victorious over
Union troops at Sabine Cross Roads near Mansfield. They were then defeated at Pleasant
Hill.

October 3. Louisiana's first Free State Legislature met.

New Orleans became the capital of the state
and remained so until 1882.

1865   February 15 or 16. The state legislature
ratified the 13th Amendment to the United
States Constitution.

March. Lieutenant Governor James M. Wells,
Democrat, became acting governor of the
state. He was subsequently elected to the
office and served until June 3, 1867, when
he was removed.

March 5. The state legislature ratified,
and the governor approved ratification of
the 15th Amendment to the United States Constitution.

May 26. The Trans-Mississippi are surrendered
to the Union forces under General E. R. S.
Canby at New Orleans.

1866   April 2. President Andrew Johnson proclaimed
that the insurrection was over in Louisiana.

Spring. The former Confederates had gained
possession of most of the local government
and the majority of the state offices. They
did not gain control of the governorship.

June 23. Former radical members of the constitutional convention were invited to attend
a meeting of the Constitutional Convention of
Louisiana which met June 26. This was part
of the attempt to remove the ex-Confederates
from their control of the state government.

July 8. Judge R. K. Howell of the Louisiana
Supreme Court, who had been elected president
of the rump constitutional convention, recon-
vened the convention of 1864 to amend the
state constitution.

July 27. Governor James M. Wells issued a
proclamation which recognized the reconvening
of the constitutional convention. The Democrats in the state were eventually forced to
accept the Reconstruction Act which required
Louisiana to accept Reconstruction.

June 3. Benjamin F. Flanders became military
governor of the state, serving until 1868.

September 27 and 28. An election was held in
the state to determine whether the Constitutional Convention should be convened, and to
elect delegates to the convention if the first
vote were favorable.

The Knights of the White Camelia were organized in New Orleans to protect and maintain
white supremacy.

1868   April. The new state constitution was adopted. It gave the vote to the Blacks and dis-
enfranchised all whites who were made ineligible to office under the proposed 14th
Amendment to the United States Constitution.

June 25. Louisiana was readmitted to the
Union. President Andrew Johnson had vetoed
the omnibus bill, but Congress overrode his
veto.

July 9. The state legislature ratified the
14th Amendment to the United States Constitution. It had previously been rejected on
December 20, 1866. Ratification of this
amendment was required before Louisiana could
be officially readmitted to the Union.

July 13. Governor Henry Clay Warmoth, Republican, was inaugurated. He served in office
until December 9, 1872.

July 18. Senators William Pitt Kellogg and
John H. Harris took their seats in the United
States Senate.

October 30. Iberia County, with its seat at
New Iberia, was established.

December 31. The Louisiana State Lottery
Company opened. The first drawing was held
January 2, 1869. This company became a major
force in the state, drawing huge profits from
the entire United States for one-quarter of a
century.

1869   March 4. Grant County was established, with
its seat at Colfax. It was named for Ulysses
S. Grant, a major general in the United States
Army during the Civil War and 18th President
of the United States.

March 6. Tangipahoa County was created, with
Amite as its seat. It was named for the
Tangipahoa Indian tribe.

Dillard University was founded and chartered
at New Orleans.

1870   Population: 726,915.

March 15. Cameron County was established,
with its seat at Cameron. It was named for
Simon Cameron, Senator from Pennsylvania,
Secretary of War in the Cabinet of President
Abraham Lincoln, and Minister to Russia.

1871   February 27. Webster County, with Minden as
its seat, was established. It was named for
Daniel Webster, Representative from New Hamp-
shire, Senator from Massachusetts, and Secretary of State in the Cabinets of Presidents
John Tyler and Millard Fillmore.

1872   December 9. Governor Henry C. Warmoth called
a special session of the new state legislature for this date. Judge E. H. Durrell
worked to prevent the session from assembling
by ordering United States Marshal S. B. Packard to seize the Mechanics Institute. Packard
occupied the State House on December 6. When
the legislature assembled Marshal Packard
refused to admit all disputed members named
by the Warmoth Board.

December 9. Pinckney B. S. Pinchbeck, Republican, became acting governor of Louisiana. He served until January 13, 1873. Governor Warmoth was impeached.

December 12. United States Attorney General George H. Williams, with the approval of President Ulysses S. Grant, recognized Pinckney B. S. Pinchbeck as the legal executive of the state.

1873   January 13. William Pitt Kellogg, Radical Republican, and John McEnery, Democrat, were both sworn in as governor at the same time. McEnery was not recognized by the United States government.

February 27. Lincoln County was established, with Ruston as its county seat. It was named for Abraham Lincoln, 16th President of the United States.

April 19. The Kellogg administration passed a civil rights act.

May 22. President Ulysses S. Grant issued a proclamation indicating his recognition of the Kellogg administration.

1874   January 4. When the state legislature met, the conservatives seized control. L. A. Wiltz was named temporary Speaker of the House. He quickly arranged for the Democrats to take control.

White Leagues were formed to fight carpetbaggers, scalawags and other whites.

1876   November. The Democrats won the state elections. The election board gave the Republicans a majority for the governor and Rutherford B. Hayes for President. The legislature was also awarded to the Republicans.

1877   January 8. Governor Stephen B. Packard, Radical Republican was sworn in. General Francis R. T. Nicholls, Democrat, was also sworn in.

March 28. East Carroll and West Carroll Counties were established. Both were named for Charles Carroll of Carrollton, Senator from Maryland and the last surviving signer of the Declaration of Independence. East Carroll

has its seat at Lake Providence, and West
Carroll at Oak Grove.

April 24. President Rutherford B. Hayes ordered all Federal troops to leave New Orleans,
thus ending reconstruction in the state.
Stephen Packard surrendered the government
of Louisiana to Francis T. Nicholls, who was
recognized as the governor of the state.
Nichols served as governor until 1880.

1878   A yellow fever epidemic occurred which led
        to the death of 4,000 people in New Orleans.

1879   James B. Eads supervised the deepening of
        the mouth of the Mississippi River so that
        New Orleans could receive ocean-going ships.
        The U. S. Army engineers completed the pro-
        ject and made the city of New Orleans an
        ocean port.

1880   Population: 939,946.

        Louis A. Wiltz, Democrat, who had been elected
        in 1879, became governor. He served in the
        office until his death in October 1881.

1881   March 5. William H. Hunt was appointed Sec-
        retary of the Navy by President James A. Gar-
        field. Hunt assumed his office as a member of
        the Cabinet on March 7, 1881.

        October. Lieutenant Governor Samuel D. McEn-
        ery, Democrat, became governor upon the death
        of Governor Louis A. Wiltz. McEnery was sub-
        sequently elected and served until 1888.

1884   Northwestern State University of Louisiana
        was established at Natchitoches.

1888   Francis T. Nichols, Democrat, became gover-
        nor of the state. He served in office until
        May 10, 1892.

1889   June 10. The United Confederate Veterans were
        organized at New Orleans to unite all the
        Confederate veteran organizations.

1890   Population: 1,118,588.

        May 10. Murphy J. Foster, Democrat, became
        governor of the state. He served in office,
        having been elected to a second term, until

May 8, 1900.

June 7. Homer Adolph Plessy set into motion
a challenge to the segregation laws when he
ignored the "colored only" sign on the coach
of the Covington and East Louisiana Railroad.
Plessy told the conductor that he was of
mixed blood. He was arrested when he refused
to leave the white coach.

1893   August 30. Huey Long was born in Winnfield,
          Louisiana.

1894   Louisiana Technical University was established
          at Ruston.

1896   May 18. Justice Henry Billings Brown gave
          the majority decision of the United States
          Supreme Court in the case of Plessy v. Fergu-
          son. The Court maintained that the "separate
          but equal" doctrine was legal. The state
          legislature may act in order to provide for
          the comforts of its people as well as the
          preservation of the public peace and order.

          Mrs. Elizabeth M. Gilmer began writing her
          personal advice column for the New Orleans
          Picayune under the name of Dorothy Dix. This
          was the first popular "advice to the lovelorn"
          column to appear in a daily newspaper.

1898   A new state constitution was adopted.

          The University of Southwestern Louisiana
          was established at Lafayette.

1900   Population: 1,381,625.

          May 8. William W. Heard, Democrat, became
          governor of the state. He served in the of-
          fice until May 10, 1904.

1901   Grambling College, an academic institution
          for Blacks, was founded at Grambling. It has
          come to be noted as one of the colleges pro-
          ducing top football players in the nation.

          Oil was discovered near Jennings and White
          Castle.

1904   May 10. Newton C. Blanchard, Democrat, be-
          came governor of the state. He served in
          the office until May 12, 1908.

Loyola University was founded and chartered at New Orleans.

1905   July. July. A "naval war" broke out between the states of Louisiana and Mississippi when the latter tried to prevent boats from New Orleans from entering its waters. A near clash occurred on August 3.

July 22. An epidemic of yellow fever broke out.

August 8. The war against mosquitoes got underway with the help of $350,000 which had been raised. Dr. J. H. White, United States Public Health Service, was in full charge.

1906   Louisiana College was established at Pineville.

1908   May 12. Jared Y. Sanders, Democrat, became governor of Louisiana. He served in the office until May 14, 1912.

July 3. La Salle County was created, with Jena as its county seat. It was named for Robert Cavalier de la Salle, the French explorer who had traveled down the Mississippi River to the Gulf of Mexico and had claimed the territory for France, naming the region Louisiana in honor of Louis XIV.

1910   Population: 1,656,388.

June 15. Evangeline County, with its seat at Ville Platte, was founded. It was named for Evangeline, the heroine of Henry Wadsworth Longfellow's poem.

St. Mary's Dominican College was founded and chartered at New Orleans.

1912   May 14. Luther E. Hall, Democrat, became governor of the state. He served in office until May 9, 1916.

June 12. The following counties were created: Allen, Beauregard, and Jefferson. Allen, with its seat at Oberlin, was named for Henry Watkins Allen, 19th governor of Louisiana. Beauregard, with its county seat at De Ridder, was named for Pierre Gustave Toutant Beauregard, a graduate of the United States Military

Academy, defender of Charleston, South Carolina who supervised the bombardment of Fort Sumter, and fought at the battle of Bull Run. Jefferson Davis County, with its seat at Jennings, was named for Jefferson Davis, Secretary of War in the Cabinet of President Franklin Pierce and President of the Confederacy.

June 28. The state legislature ratified the 16th Amendment to the United States Constitution.

1914   June 5. The state legislature ratified the 17th Amendment to the United States Constitution.

1916   May 9. Ruffin G. Pleasant, Democrat, became governor of Louisiana. He served in the office until May 11, 1920.

1917   At the insistence of the United States Navy, "Storyville" or "The District," a part of New Orleans which was set aside for organized vice was closed down. This closing tended to drive the jazz musicians who made a living in the honky-tonk and sporting houses out of New Orleans.

The New Orleans Baptist Theological Seminary was established in New Orleans.

1918   August 9. Governor Pleasant approved the ratification of the 18th Amendment to the United States Constitution which had been previously passed by the state legislature.

Huey Long was elected railroad commissioner for the North Louisiana District.

1920   Population: 1,798,509.

May 11. John M. Parker, Democrat, became governor of the state. He served in the gubernatorial office until May 13, 1924.

1921   Louisiana adopted a new constitution, its tenth. Its object was to maintain the safeguards of "white supremacy."

1922   The first radio stations in the state began broadcasting. They were WWL at New Orleans and KEEL at Shreveport.

1923   The Notre Dame Seminary Graduate School of
Theology was founded and chartered at New
Orleans.

1924   May 13. Henry L. Fuqua, Democrat, became
governor of Louisiana. He served in the office until his death on October 11, 1926.

1925   Southeastern Louisiana University was established at Hammond. Xavier University of
Louisiana was founded at New Orleans.

1926   October 11. Lieutenant Governor Oramel H.
Simpson, Democrat, became governor of the
state, upon the death of Governor Henry L.
Fuqua. Simpson served until the end of the
term on May 21, 1928.

1927   The Mississippi River flooded and drove
some 300,000 people from their homes. The
flood caused huge property damages.

1928   May 21. Huey P. Long, Jr., Democrat, became
governor of the state. He resigned his position on January 25, 1932.

            Northeast Louisiana University was established
at Monroe.

1929   Huey P. Long, governor of the state, was impeached by the Louisiana House of Representatives, but he was not convicted.

1930   Population: 2,101,593.

            Governor Huey P. Long ran for the United
States Senate and was elected.

1932   January 25. Lieutenant Governor Alvin O.
King, Democrat, became governor of the state
upon the resignation of Governor Huey P.
Long. King served in the office until the
end of the term on May 10, 1932.

            May 10. Oscar K. Allen, Democrat, became
governor of the state and served until his
death on January 28, 1936.

            August. Huey Long compaigned in Arkansas and
virtually singlehandedly helped to elect
Hattie Caraway to the United States Senate.

1933   Huey P. Long published his autobiography,

Every Man a King.

1935   September 8. Huey P. Long, who had become
       powerful both in Louisiana and national po-
       litics, was shot to death in the corridor
       of the state capitol building in Baton Rouge,
       Louisiana, by Dr. Carl Austin Weiss, Jr., a
       young idealist. Long died two days later
       on September 10.

1936   January 28. Lieutenant Governor James A.
       Noe, Democrat, became governor of Louisiana
       upon the death of Governor Oscar K. Allen.
       Noe served until the end of the term on May
       12, 1936.

       May 12. Richard W. Leche, Democrat, became
       governor of Louisiana and served in office
       until his resignation on June 26, 1939.

       Earl Long was elected lieutenant
       governor of the state.

1938   Our Lady of Holy Cross College was estab-
       lished at New Orleans.

1939   June 26. Lieutenant Governor Earl K. Long,
       Democrat, became governor of the state upon
       the resignation of Richard W. Leche. He
       served until May 14, 1940.

1940   Population: 2,363,880.

       May 14. Sam H. Jones, Democrat, became
       governor of Louisiana. He served in the gu-
       bernatorial office until May 9, 1944.

1944   May 9. James H. Davis, Democrat, became
       governor of the state. He served in the of-
       fice until May 11, 1948.

       Earl Long was defeated in his campaign for
       the position of lieutenant governor of the
       state.

       New Orleans opened International House as a
       means of helping to increase its share of
       foreign trade.

1948   May 11. Earl K. Long, Democrat, became gov-
       ernor of the state. He served in the office
       until May 13, 1952.

In addition to Earl Long's election as
governor Russell Long was elected Senator.

WDSO-TV of New Orleans began broadcasting as
the first television station in the state.

1950   Population: 2,683,516.

May 17. The state legislature ratified the
22nd Amendment to the United States Constitution.

1952   The case of <u>Bush v. Orleans Parish School
Board</u> was reactivated.

May 13. Robert F. Kennon, Democrat, became
governor of the state. He served in the
office until May 8, 1956.

1954   May 17. Louisiana's segregation program was
challenged as a result of the unanimous
United States Supreme Court decision in the
case of <u>Brown v. Board of Education of Topeka</u>
which reversed the "separate but equal" doc-
trine of <u>Plessy v. Ferguson</u>.

July 6. The state legislature completed
passage of a plan for a constitutional amendment and legislation which would permit the
use of the state's police power to maintain
segregated public schools. The voters approved the amendment on November 2.

November 13. Governor Kennan made a statement
at the Southern Governors Conference at Boca
Raton, Florida, indicating that segregation
was dangerous, and that he would attempt to
uphold state control of school policy.

1955   August 19. Archbishop Joseph Francis Rummel
stated that desegregation of parochial
schools would occur within a year. However,
the Archbishop held back his plans because
he learned that the legislature had plans to
deprive the Catholic schools of free lunches
and free textbooks, as well as putting church
property on the tax rolls if integration was
begun in the parochial schools.

1956   February 15. In the case of <u>Bush v. Orleans
Parish School Board</u>, the federal court at
New Orleans ruled that all state laws sup-
porting segregation were contrary to the

1954 United States Supreme Court decision of
Brown v. Board of Education of Topeka. The
school board was ordered to proceed with
"all deliberate speed" to desegregate the
public schools of New Orleans.

May 9. Earl K. Long, Democrat, again became
governor of Louisiana. He served in the office until the end of his term on May 10,
1960. Long was ill, and before the end of
his term he was committed to a mental hospital in Texas by his wife supported by Russell
Long. Earl was eventually released and returned to his work.

July 16. Governor Earl Long signed a bill
banning inter-racial athletic contests and
social events. The law took effect October
15.

Nicholls State University was founded and
chartered at Thibodaux.

The Citizens' Council group published a pam-
phlet entitled Voter Qualification Laws in
Louisiana -- The Key to Our Victory. It contained a blueprint indicating how the polls
could be purged of Blacks and instructions on
how Blacks could be prevented from registering.

The state legislature passed eight acts to
strengthen segregation. Except for three
which provided for the dismissal of teachers,
school employees and school bus drivers who
urged integration, the remainder were declared unconstitutional.

1957   June 27-28. Hurricane Audrey and a subsequent tidal wave hit the gulf coasts of
Louisiana and Texas. 531 people were left
dead or missing.

1958   The state legislature passed six additional
segregation acts, including one which authorized the closing of desegregated schools.
They were later held unconstitutional.

1959   May 25. The United States Supreme Court declared unconstitutional a state ban on boxing
matches between Black and white boxers.

June 19. Governor Earl Long was committed
to a state mental hospital in Texas. Lieutenant Governor Lether Frazar became acting
governor of Louisiana.

1960   Population: 3,257,022.

May 1. Federal Judge Skelly Wright ordered
a plan for desegregation of the New Orleans
public schools by this date. Judge Wright
granted a delay until November 14.

May 10. James H. Davis, Democrat, again became governor of the state. He served until
May 12, 1964.

November 17. New Orleans was the scene of
some of the worst anti-integration riots since
the beginning of school integration there.

Earl Long ran for lieutenant governor of the
state. He also ran for Congress from his
central Louisiana district.

1961   The National Aeronautics and Space Administration chose the Michaud Ordnance Plant, later the Michaud Assembly Facility, in New
Orleans for the production of saturn rocket
boosters.

1962   January 16 - February 1. Student demonstra-
tions occurred at Southern University, the
all-Black college in Baton Rouge. The University was closed from January 18 to 28.

February 19. The United States Supreme Court
upheld a ruling which declared unconstitutional a 1961 Louisiana law permitting the closing of the public schools in school districts
which were under Federal orders to integrate
a ruling made by a three-judge United States
court in New Orleans, August 30, 1961.

March 27. Archbishop Joseph Francis Rummel
ordered all Roman Catholic schools in the
New Orleans diocese to desegregate.

1963   October 8. The Justice Department sued in
the United States District Court in Baton
Rouge, Louisiana in order to prevent the use
of a voter registration form which was used
as a test to discriminate against Blacks.

The Mississippi River-Gulf Outlet, a 76-mile short cut from New Orleans to the sea was opened.

1964 January 13. The United States Supreme Court unanimously held as unconstitutional a state law which required that the race of all political candidates be printed on the ballot.

May 12. John J. McKeithen, Democrat, became governor of Louisiana. He served in the office until May 9, 1972.

July 9. The New Orleans Cotton Exchange, the second largest in the United States, stopped "futures" trading after 93 years of operation. It announced that its action was due to government control which was exercised by the Agricultural Act of 1964.

November 3. A code of ethics for state officials was adopted.

Two Republicans were elected to the Louisiana legislature for the first time since the Reconstruction era.

1965 The Supreme Court held a state law requiring voter registration applicants to pass a test interpreting the state and federal constitutions unconstitutional.

1966 July 5. The state legislature ratified the 25th Amendment to the United States Constitution.

November 8. An amendment to the state constitution was passed allowing the governor to serve two consecutive terms.

1968 January 15. The United States Supreme Court upheld a lower federal court decision that the state program of tuition grants for students was unconstitutional.

1969 St. Joseph Seminary College was established at St. Benedict.

1970 Population: 3,641,306.

1971 April 17. The state legislature ratified the 26th Amendment to the United States Constitution.

May 9. Edwin W. Edwards, Democrat, became
governor of the state.

July 5. Governor Edwards signed a series of
bills which repealed the state's holdover
segregation laws.

1973   November 13. The public college desegregation plan submitted by Louisiana was rejected
by the Department of Health, Education and
Welfare.

1974   April 20. The voters approved the 11th constitution of the state. It was to go into
effect in 1975.

1975   January 1. The new constitution became ef-
fective, ending property taxes for homes
of $30,000 or less.

The state legislature defeated the Equal
Rights Amendment to the United States Constitution.

1976   May. President Valery Giscard d'Estaing of
France visited New Orleans and Lafayette
as part of his state visit to the United
States.

June. Rotary International held its 67th
annual convention in New Orleans.

July 2. The United States Supreme Court
voted 5-4 to strike down the state's capital punishment law.

August 12. An explosion occurred in a
30-story refining tower of the Tenneco
Oil Company in Chalmette. 12 men were
killed and five others were seriously
injured.

1977   June 6. The Supreme Court ruled that states
could not impose an automatic death penalty
for the killing of police officers in re-
viewing a Louisiana law.

June 23. The state legislature passed a
bill legalizing the manufacture and sale
of the controversial cancer cure, laetrile.

BIOGRAPHICAL DIRECTORY

The selected list of governors, United States Senators and Members of the House of Representatives for
Louisiana, 1812-1970, includes all persons listed in
the Chronology for whom basic biographical data was
readily available. Older biographical sources are frequently in conflict on certain individuals, and in such
cases the source most commonly cited by later authorities was preferred.

ACKLEN, Joseph Hayes
Democrat
b. Nashville, Tenn., May 20, 1850
d. Nashville, Tenn., September 28, 1938
U. S. Representative, 1878-81

ALLEN, Asa Leonard
Democrat
b. near Winnfield, La., January 5, 1891
d. Winnfield, La., January 5, 1869
U. S. Representative, 1849-53

ALLEN, Henry W.
Sectional Democrat
b. Prince Edward County, Va., April 29, 1820
d. April 22, 1866
Governor of Louisiana, 1864-65

ALLEN, Oscar K.
Democrat
d. January 28, 1936
Governor of Louisiana, 1932-36

ASWELL, James Benjamin
Democrat
b. near Vernon, La., December 23, 1869
d. Washington, D. C., March 16, 1931
U. S. Representative, 1913-31

BAIRD, Samuel Thomas
Democrat
b. Oak Ridge, La., May 5, 1861
d. Washington, D. C., April 22, 1899
U. S. Representative, 1897-99

BAKER, Joshua
Provisional Governor of Louisiana, 1868

BARROW, Alexander
Whig
b. Nashville, Tenn., March 27, 1801
d. Baltimore, Md., December 19, 1846
U. S. Senator, 1841-46

BEAUVAIS, Armand
National Republican
Governor of Louisiana, 1829-30

BENJAMIN, Judah Philip
    Democrat
    b. on the island of St. Croix, Danish West
        Indies, August 6, 1811
    d. Paris, France, May 8, 1884
    U. S. Senator, 1853-59 (Whig), 1859-61 (Democrat)

BLACKBURN, William Jasper
    Republican
    b. Fourche de Mau, Ark., July 24, 1820
    d. Little Rock, Ark., November 10, 1899
    U. S. Representative, 1868-69

BLANCHARD, Newton Crain
    Democrat
    b. Rapides Parish, La., January 29, 1849
    d. Shreveport, La., June 22, 1922
    U. S. Representative, 1881-94
    U. S. Senator, 1894-97
    Governor of Louisiana, 1904-08

BOARMAN, Alexander (Aleck)
    Liberal
    b. Yazoo City, Miss., December 10, 1839
    d. Loon Lake, N. Y., August 30, 1916
    U. S. Representative, 1872-73

BOATNER, Charles Jahleah
    Democrat
    b. Columbia, La., January 23, 1849
    d. New Orleans, La., March 21, 1903
    U. S. Representative, 1889-95, 1896-97

BOGGS, Thomas Hale, Sr.
    Democrat
    b. Long Beach, Miss., February 15, 1914
    U. S. Representative, 1941-43, 1947-

BOULIGNY, Charles Joseph Dominique
    b. New Orleans, La., August 22, 1773
    d. New Orleans, La., March 6, 1833
    U. S. Senator, 1824-29

BOULIGNY, John Edward
    b. New Orleans, La., February 5, 1824
    d. Washington, D. C., February 20, 1864
    U. S. Representative, 1859-61

BREAZEALE, Phanor
    Democrat
    b. Natchitoches, La., December 29, 1858
    d. Natchitoches, La., April 29, 1934
    U. S. Representative, 1899-1905

BRENT, William Leigh
    b. Port Tobacco, Md., February 20, 1784
    d. St. Matinsville, La., July 7, 1848
    U. S. Representative, 1823-29

BROOKS, Overton
    Democrat
    b. near Baton Rouge, La., December 21, 1897
    d. Bethesda, Md., September 16, 1961
    U. S. Representative, 1937-61

BROUSSARD, Edward Sidney
    Democrat
    b. near Loreauville, La., December 4, 1874
    d. New Iberia, La., November 19, 1934
    U. S. Senator, 1921-33

BROUSSARD, Robert Foligny
    Democrat
    b. on Mary Louise Plantation, near New Iberia,
        La., August 17, 1864
    d. New Iberia, La., April 12, 1918
    U. S. Representative, 1897-1915
    U. S. Senator, 1915-18

BROWN, James
    b. near Staunton, Va., September 11, 1776
    d. Philadelphia, Pa., April 7, 1835
    U. S. Senator, 1813-17, 1819-23

BUCK, Charles Francis
    Democrat
    b. Durrheim, Grand Duchy of Baden, Germany,
        November 5, 1841
    d. New Orleans, La., January 19, 1918
    U. S. Representative, 1895-97

BULLARD, Henry Adams
    Whig
    b. Pepperell, Mass., September 9, 1788
    d. New Orleans, La., April 17, 1851
    U. S. Representative, 1831-34, 1850-51

BUTLER, Thomas
    b. near Carlisle, Pa., April 14, 1785
    d. St. Louis, Mo., August 7, 1847
    U. S. Representative, 1818-21

CAFFERY, Donelson
    b. near Franklin, La., September 10, 1835
    d. New Orleans, La., December 30, 1906
    U. S. Senator, 1892-1901

CAFFERY, Patrick Thomson
    Democrat
    b. near Franklin, La., July 6, 1932
    U. S. Representative, 1969-

CHINN, Thomas Withers
    Whig
    b. near Cynthiana, Ky., November 22, 1791
    d. at his plantation, West Baton Rouge Parish,
        La., May 22, 1852
    U. S. Representative, 1839-41

CLAIBORNE, William Charles Coe
    Jefferson Democrat (Tennessee)
    Democrat (Louisiana)
    b. Surrey County, Va., 1775
    d. New Orleans, La., November 23, 1817
    U. S. Representative, 1797-1801 (Tennessee)
    Governor of Territory of Mississippi, 1801-03
    Governor of Territory of Orleans, 1804-12
    Governor of Louisiana, 1812-16
    U. S. Senator, 1817 (Louisiana)

CLARK, Daniel
    ---- (Orleans)
    b. Sligo, Ireland, about 1766
    d. New Orleans, La., August 16, 1813
    U. S. Representative (Territorial Delegate),
        1806-09

COLEMAN, Hamilton Dudley
    Republican
    b. New Orleans, La., May 12, 1845
    d. Biloxi, Miss., March 16, 1926
    U. S. Representative, 1889-91

CONRAD, Charles Mynn
    Whig
    b. Winchester, Va., December 24, 1804
    d. New Orleans, La., February 11, 1878
    U. S. Senator, 1842-43
    U. S. Representative, 1849-50
    U. S. Secretary of War, 1850-53

DARRALL, Chester Bidwell
    Republican
    b. near Addison, Pa., June 24, 1842
    d. Washington, D. C., January 1, 1908
    U. S. Representative, 1869-78, 1881-83

DAVEY, Robert Charles
    Democrat
    b. New Orleans, La., October 22, 1853

d. New Orleans, La., December 26, 1908
U. S. Representative, 1893-95, 1897-1908

DAVIDSON, Thomas Green
Democrat
b. Coles Creek, Miss., August 3, 1805
d. Springfield, La., September 11, 1883
U. S. Representative, 1855-61

DAVIS, James H.
Democrat
b. Quitman, La., September 11, 1902
Governor of Louisiana, 1944-48, 1960-64

DAWSON, John Bennett
Democrat
b. near Nashville, Tenn., March 17, 1798
d. St. Francisville, La., June 26, 1845
U. S. Representative, 1841-45

DEAR, Cleveland
Democrat
b. Sugartown, La., August 22, 1888
d. Alexandria, La., December 30, 1950
U. S. Representative, 1933-37

DERBIGNY, Pierre
National Republican
b. France, 1767
d. October 6, 1829
Governor, 1828-29

DE ROWEN, Rene Louis
Democrat
b. near Ville Platte, La., January 7, 1874
d. Baton Rouge, La., March 27, 1942
U. S. Representative, 1927-41

DESTREHAN, John Noel
b. in what later became St. Charles Parish,
     La., 1780
d. (near Destrehan, La.), 1824
U. S. Senator, 1812

DOWNS, Solomon Weathersbee
Democrat
b. Montgomery County, Tenn., 1801
d. Crab Orchard Springs, Ky., August 14, 1854
U. S. Senator, 1847-53

DUNBAR, William
Democrat
b. Virginia, 1805

d. on his plantation in the Parish of St.
    Bernard, La., March 18, 1861
U. S. Representative, 1853-55

DUPRE, Henry Garland
    Democrat
    b. Opelousas, La., July 28, 1873
    d. Washington, D. C., February 21, 1924
    U. S. Representative, 1910-24

DUPRE, Jacques
    National Republican
    Governor of Louisiana, 1830-31

EDWARDS, Edwin Washington
    Democrat
    b. Avoyelles Parish, near Marksville, La.,
        August 7, 1927
    U. S. Representative, 1965-72
    Governor of Louisiana, 1972-

ELAM, Joseph Barton
    b. near Hope, Ark., June 12, 1821
    d. Mansfield, La., July 4, 1885
    U. S. Representative, 1877-81

ELDER, James Walter
    b. Grand Prairie, Tex., October 5, 1882
    d. Ruston, La., December 16, 1941
    U. S. Representative, 1913-15

ELLENDER, Allen Joseph
    Democrat
    b. Montegut, La., September 24, 1891
    U. S. Senator, 1937-
        President pro tempore, 1971-

ELLIS, Ezekiel John
    Democrat
    b. Covington, La., October 15, 1840
    d. Washington, D. C., April 25, 1889
    U. S. Representative, 1875-85

ESTOPINAL, Albert
    Democrat
    b. St. Bernard Parish, La., January 30, 1845
    d. New Orleans, La., April 28, 1919
    U. S. Representative, 1908-19

EUSTIS, George, Jr.
    American Party
    b. New Orleans, La., September 28, 1828
    d. Cannes, France, March 15, 1872

U. S. Representative, 1855-59

EUSTIS, James Biddle
  Democrat
  b. New Orleans, La., August 27, 1834
  d. Newport, R. I., September 9, 1899
  U. S. Senator, 1876-79, 1885-91

FAVROT, George Kent
  Democrat
  b. Baton Rouge, La., November 20, 1868
  d. Baton Rouge, La., December 26, 1934
  U. S. Representative, 1907-09, 1921-25

FEAZEL, William Crosson
  Democrat
  b. near Farmerville, La., June 10, 1895
  d. Shreveport, La., March 16, 1965
  U. S. Senator, 1948

FERNANDEZ, Joachin Octave
  Democrat
  b. New Orleans, La., August 14, 1896
  U. S. Representative, 1931-41

FLANDERS, Benjamin Franklin
  Unionist
  b. Bristol, N. H., January 26, 1816
  d. at his estate "Ben Alva," near Youngsville,
      La., March 13, 1896
  U. S. Representative, 1862-63
  Military Governor of Louisiana, 1867-68

FOSTER, Murphy James
  Democrat
  b. Franklin, La., January 12, 1849
  d. at Dixie Plantation, near Franklin, La.,
      June 12, 1921
  Governor of Louisiana, 1892-1900
  U. S. Senator, 1901-13

FROMENTIN, Eligius
  b. France
  d. New Orleans, La., October 6, 1822
  U. S. Senator, 1813-19

FUQUA, Henry L.
  Democrat
  b. Baton Rouge, La., November 8, 1865
  d. October 11, 1926
  Governor of Louisiana, 1924-26

GARLAND, Rice
    Whig
    b. Lynchburg, Va., about 1795
    d. Brownsville, Tex., 1861
    U. S. Representative, 1834-40

GAY, Edward James
    Democrat
    b. Liberty, Va., February 3, 1816
    d. on St. Louis Plantation, Iberville Parish,
        La., May 30, 1889
    U. S. Representative, 1885-89

GAY, Edward James (grandson of the preceding)
    b. Union plantation, Iberville Parish, La.,
        May 5, 1878
    d. New Orleans, La., December 1, 1952
    U. S. Senator, 1918-21

GIBSON, Randall Lee
    Democrat
    b. Spring Hill, near Versailles, Ky., September
        10, 1832
    d. Hot Springs, Ark., December 15, 1892
    U. S. Representative, 1875-83
    U. S. Senator, 1883-92

GILMORE, Samuel Louis
    Democrat
    b. New Orleans, La., July 30, 1859
    d. Abita Springs, La., July 18, 1910
    U. S. Representative, 1909-10

GRIFFITH, John Keller
    Democrat
    b. Port Hudson, La., October 16, 1882
    d. Slidell, La., September 25, 1942
    U. S. Representative, 1937-41

GUION, Walter
    Democrat
    b. near Thibodaux, La., April 3, 1849
    d. New Orleans, La., February 7, 1927
    U. S. Senator, 1918

GURLEY, Henry Hosford
    Whig
    b. Lebanon, Mass., May 20, 1788
    d. Baton Rouge, La., March 16, 1833
    U. S. Representative, 1823-31

HAHN, Michael
    Republican

b. Bavaria, Germany, November 24, 1830
d. Washington, D. C., March 15, 1886
U. S. Representative, 1862-63 (Unionist)
Governor of Louisiana, 1864-65
U. S. Representative, 1885-86 (Republican)

HALL, Luther E.
b. Morehouse Parish, La., August 30, 1869
d. November 6, 1921
Governor of Louisiana, 1912-16

HARMANSON, John Henry
Democrat
b. Norfolk, Va., January 15, 1803
d. New Orleans, La., October 24, 1850
U. S. Representative, 1845-50

HARRIS, John Spafford
Republican
b. Truxton, N. Y., December 18, 1825
d. Butte, Mont., January 25, 1906
U. S. Senator, 1868-71

HEARD, William W.
Democrat
b. Union Parish, La., April 28, 1853
d. June 1, 1926
Governor of Louisiana, 1900-04

HEBERT, Felix Edward
Democrat
b. New Orleans, La., October 12, 1901
U. S. Representative, 1941-

HEBERT, Paul O.
b. Iberville Parish, La., December 12, 1818
d. August 29, 1880
Governor of Louisiana, 1853-56

HUNT, Carleton
b. New Orleans, La., January 1, 1836
d. New Orleans, La., August 14, 1921
U. S. Representative, 1883-85

HUNT, Theodore Gaillard
Whig
b. Charleston, S. C., October 23, 1805
d. New Orleans, La., November 15, 1893
U. S. Representative, 1853-55

IRION, Alfred Briggs
Democrat
b. near Evergreen, La., February 18, 1833

d. New Orleans, La., May 21, 1903
U. S. Representative, 1885-87

IRWIN, Edward Michael
Republican
b. near Leasburg, Mo., April 14, 1869
d. Belleville, Ill., January 30, 1933
U. S. Representative, 1925-31

JOHNSON, Henry
Whig
b. Virginia, September 14, 1783
d. Parish of Pointe Coupee, La., September
   4, 1864
U. S. Senator, 1818-24
Governor of Louisiana, 1824-28
U. S. Representative, 1834-39
U. S. Senator, 1844-49

JOHNSON, Isaac
Democrat
Governor of Louisiana, 1846-50

JOHNSTON, Josiah Stoddard
Democrat
b. Salisbury, Conn., November 24, 1784
d. as a result of an explosion on a steamboat
   Lioness on the Red River in La., May 19,
   1833
U. S. Representative, 1821-23
U. S. Senator, 1824-33

JONAS, Benjamin Franklin
Democrat
b. Williamsport, Ky., July 19, 1834
d. New Orleans, La., December 21, 1911
U. S. Senator, 1879-85

JONES, Roland
Democrat
b. Salisbury, N. C., November 18, 1813
d. Shreveport, La., February 5, 1869
U. S. Representative, 1853-55

JONES, Sam H.
Democrat
Governor of Louisiana, 1940-44

KELLOGG, William Pitt
Republican
b. Orwell, Vt., December 8, 1831
d. Washington, D. C., August 10, 1918
U. S. Senator, 1868-72

Governor of Louisiana, 1873-77
U. S. Senator, 1877-83
U. S. Representative, 1883-85

KEMP, Bolivar Edwards
Democrats
b. on Kemp homestead near Amite, La., December
    28, 1871
d. Amite, La., June 19, 1933
U. S. Representative, 1925-33

KENNON, Robert F.
Democrat
Governor of Lousiana, 1952-56

KING, Alvin O.
Democrat
b. Leoti, Kans., June 21, 1890
d. February 21, 1958
Governor of Louisiana, 1932

KING, John Floyd
Democrat
b. St. Simons Island, off the coast of Georgia,
    April 20, 1842
d. Washington, D. C., May 8, 1915
U. S. Representative, 1879-87

LA BRANCHE, Alcée Louis
Democrat
b. near New Orleans, La., 1806
d. Hot Springs, Va., August 17, 1861
U. S. Representative, 1843-45

LAGAN, Matthew Diamond
Democrat
b. Maghena, Londonderry, Ireland, June 20,
    1829
d. New Orleans, La., April 8, 1901
U. S. Representative, 1887-89, 1891-93

LANDRY, Joseph Aristide
Whig
b. near Donaldsonville, La., July 10, 1817
d. near Donaldsonville, La., March 9, 1881
U. S. Representative, 1851-53

LARCADE, Henry Dominique, Jr.
Democrat
b. Opelousas, La., July 12, 1890
d. Opelousas, La., March 14, 1966
U. S. Representative, 1943-53

LA SERE, Emile
    Democrat
    b. Isle of Santo Domingo, 1802
    d. New Orleans, La., August 14, 1882
    U. S. Representative, 1846-51

LAWRENCE, Effingham
    Democrat
    b. Bayside, near Flushing, Long Island, N. Y.,
        March 2, 1826
    d. Magnolia Plantation, Plaquemines Parish, La.,
        December 9, 1878
    U. S. Representative, 1875

LAZARO, Ladislas
    Democrat
    b. near Ville Platte, La., June 5, 1872
    d. Washington, D. C., March 30, 1927
    U. S. Representative, 1913-27

LECHE, Richard W.
    Democrat
    b. New Orleans, La., May 17, 1898
    d. February 1965
    Governor of Louisiana, 1936-39

LEONARD, John Edwards
    Republican
    b. Fairville, Pa., September 22, 1845
    d. Habana, Cuba, March 15, 1878
    U. S. Representative, 1877-78

LEVY, William Mallory
    Democrat
    b. Isle of Wight, Va., October 31, 1827
    d. Saratoga, N. Y., August 14, 1882
    U. S. Representative, 1875-77

LEWIS, Edward Taylor
    Democrat
    b. Opelousas, La., October 26, 1834
    d. Opelousas, La., April 26, 1927
    U. S. Representative, 1883-85

LIVINGSTON, Edward
    Democrat (New York - Louisiana)
    b. Clermont, Livingston Manor, N. Y.,
        May 26, 1764
    d. "Montgomery Place" on the Hudson River,
        Barrytown, N. Y., May 23, 1836
    U. S. Representative, 1795-1801 (New York),
        1823-29 (Louisiana)
    U. S. Senator, 1829-31 (Louisiana)
    U. S. Secretary of State, 1831-33

LONG, Earl K.
    Democrat
    b. Winnfield, La., August 26, 1895
    d. September 5, 1960
    Governor of Louisiana, 1939-40, 1948-52,
        1956-60

LONG, George Shannon
    Democrat
    b. Tunica, La., seven miles from Winnfield,
        La., September 11, 1883
    d. Bethesda, Md., March 22, 1958
    U. S. Representative, 1953-58

LONG, Gillis William
    Democrat
    b. Winnfield, La., May 4, 1923
    U. S. Representative, 1963-65

LONG, Huey Pierce
    Democrat
    b. near Winnfield, La., August 30, 1893
    d. as a result of gunshot wounds at the state
        Capitol Building, Baton Rouge, La., Sep-
        tember 10, 1935
    Governor of Louisiana, 1928-32
    U. S. Senator, 1932-35

LONG, Rose McConnell
    Democrat
    b. Greensburg, Ind., April 8, 1892
    d. Boulder, Colo., May 27, 1920
    U. S. Senator, 1936-37

LONG, Russell Billiu
    Democrat
    b. Shreveport, La., November 3, 1918
    U. S. Senator, 1948

LONG, Speedy Oteria
    Democrat
    b. Tullos, La., June 16, 1928
    U. S. Representative, 1965-

MAGRUDER, Allan Bowie
    Democrat
    b. Kentucky, 1775
    d. Opelousas, La., April 16, 1822

MALONEY, Paul Herbert
    Democrat
    b. New Orleans, La., February 14, 1876
    d. New Orleans, La., March 26, 1967

U. S. Representative, 1931-40, 1943-47

MANN, James
Democrat
b. Gorham, Maine, June 22, 1822
d. New Orleans, La., August 26, 1868
U. S. Representative, 1868

MARTIN, Whitmell Pugh
Democrat
b. near Napoleonville, La., August 12, 1867
d. Washington, D. C., April 6, 1929
U. S. Representative, 1915-19 (Progressive),
    1919-29 (Democrat)

MCCLEERY, James
Republican
b. Mecca Township, Ohio, December 2, 1837
d. New York, N. Y., November 5, 1871
U. S. Representative, 1871

MCENERY, Samuel Douglas
Democrat
b. Monroe, La., May 28, 1837
d. New Orleans, La., June 28, 1910
Governor of Louisiana, 1881-88
U. S. Senator, 1897-1910

MCKEITHEN, John J.
Democrat
Governor of Louisiana, 1964-72

MCKENZIE, Charles Edgar
Democrat
b. Pelican, La., October 3, 1896
d. Monroe, La., June 7, 1956
U. S. Representative, 1943-47

MCSWEEN, Harold Barnett
Democrat
b. Alexandria, La., July 19, 1926
U. S. Representative, 1959-63

MEYER, Adolph
Democrat
b. Natchez, Miss., October 19, 1842
d. New Orleans, La., March 8, 1908
U. S. Representative, 1891-1908

MILLS, Newt Virgus
Democrat
b. Calhoun, La., September 27, 1894
U. S. Representative, 1937-43

MONTET, Numa Francais
     Democrat
     b. Thibodaux, La., September 17, 1892
     U. S. Representative, 1929-37

MOORE, John
     Whig
     b. Berkeley, Va., 1788
     d. Franklin, La., June 17, 1867
     U. S. Representative, 1840-43, 1851-53

MOORE, Thomas O.
     Democrat
     b. Sampson County, N. C., April 10, 1804
     d. June 25, 1876
     Governor of Louisiana, 1860-64

MOREY, Frank
     Republican
     b. Boston, Mass., July 11, 1840
     d. Washington, D. C., September 22, 1889
     U. S. Representative, 1869-76

MORGAN, Lewis Lovering
     Democrat
     b. Mandeville, La., March 2, 1876
     d. New Orleans, La., June 10, 1950
     U. S. Representative, 1912-17

MORRISON, James Hobson
     Democrat
     b. Hammond, La., December 8, 1908
     U. S. Representative, 1943-67

MORSE, Isaac Edward
     Democrat
     b. Attakapas, La., May 22, 1809
     d. New Orleans, La., February 11, 1866
     U. S. Representative, 1844-51

MOUTON, Alexander
     Democrat
     b. Attakapas district in what is now Lafayette
          Parish, La., November 19, 1804
     d. near Vermillionville (now Lafayette),
          Vt., February 12, 1885
     U. S. Senator, 1837-42
     Governor of Louisiana, 1842-46

MOUTON, Robert Louis
     Democrat
     b. Duchamp, La., October 20, 1892
     d. New Orleans, La., November 26, 1956

U. S. Representative, 1937-41

NASH, Charles Edmund
    Republican
    b. Opelousas, La., May 23, 1844
    d. New Orleans, La., June 2, 1913
    U. S. Representative, 1875-77

NEWSHAM, Joseph Parkinson
    Republican
    b. Preston, England, May 24, 1837
    d. St. Francisville, La., October 22, 1919
    U. S. Representative, 1868-69, 1870-71

NEWTON, Cherubusco
    Democrat
    b. Greenburg, La., May 15, 1848
    d. Monroe, La., May 26, 1910
    U. S. Representative, 1887-89

NICHOLAS, Robert Carter
    Democrat
    b. Hanover, Va., 1793
    d. Terrebonne, La., December 24, 1857
    U. S. Senator, 1836-41

NICHOLLS, Francis T.
    Democrat
    b. Donaldsonville, La., August 20, 1834
    d. 1912
    Governor of Louisiana, 1877-80, 1888-92

NOE, James A.
    Democrat
    Governor of Louisiana, 1936

O'CONNOR, James
    Democrat
    b. New Orleans, La., April 4, 1870
    d. Covington, La., January 7, 1941
    U. S. Representative, 1919-31

OGDEN, Henry Warren
    Democrat
    b. Abingdon, Va., October 21, 1842
    d. Benton, La., July 23, 1905
    U. S. Representative, 1894-99

OVERTON, John Holmes
    Democrat
    b. Marksville, La., September 17,
        1875
    d. Bethesda, Md., May 14, 1948
    U. S. Representative, 1931-33
    U. S. Senator, 1933-48

OVERTON, Walter Hampden
    Democrat
    b. near Louisa Court House, Va., 1788
    d. near Alexandria, Pa., December 24, 1845
    U. S. Representative, 1829-31

PARKER, John M.
    Independent Democrat
    b. Bethel Church, Miss., March 16, 1863
    d. May 20, 1939
    Governor of Louisiana, 1920-24

PASSMAN, Otto Ernest
    Democrat
    b. near Franklinton, La., June 27, 1900
    U. S. Representative, 1947

PENN, Alexander Gordon
    Democrat
    b. near Stella, Va., May 10, 1799
    d. Washington, D. C., May 7, 1866
    U. S. Representative, 1850-53

PERKINS, John, Jr.
    Democrat
    b. Natchez, Miss., July 1, 1819
    d. Baltimore, Md., November 28, 1885
    U. S. Representative, 1853-55

PINCHBACK, Pinckney B. S.
    Republican
    b. Macon, Ga., May 10, 1837
    d. December 21, 1921
    Governor of Louisiana, 1872-73

PLEASANT, Ruffin G.
    Democrat
    b. Shiloh, La., June 2, 1871
    d, September 12, 1937
    Governor of Louisiana, 1916-20

PLAUCHE, Vance Gabriel
    b. Plaucheville, August 25, 1897
    U. S. Representative, 1941-43

PORTER, Alexander
    Whig
    b. near Armagh, Ireland, 1786
    d. Attakapas, La., January 13, 1844
    U. S. Senator, 1833-37

POSEY, Thomas
   b. Fairfax, Va., July 9, 1750
   d. Shawneetown, Ill., March 19, 1818
   U. S. Senator, 1812-13
   Governor of Indiana Territory, 1813-16

POYDRAS, Julien de Lallande
   (Orleans)
   b. Nantes, France, April 3, 1740
   d. Point Coupee, La., June 14, 1824
   U. S. Representative (Territorial Delegate),
      1809-11

PRICE, Andrew
   Democrat
   b. Chatsworth Plantation, near Franklin, La.,
      April 2, 1854
   d. Acadia Plantation, Lafourche Parish, La.,
      February 5, 1909
   U. S. Representative, 1889-97

PUJO, Arsene Paulin
   Democrat
   b. near Lake Charles, La., December 16, 1861
   d. New Orleans, La., December 31, 1939
   U. S. Representative, 1903-13

RANSDELL, Joseph Eugene
   Democrat
   b. Alexandria, La., October 7, 1858
   d. Lake Providence, La., July 27, 1954
   U. S. Representative, 1889-1913
   U. S. Senator, 1913-31

RARICK, John Richard
   Democrat
   b. Waterford, Ind., January 29, 1924
   U. S. Representative, 1967-

RIPLEY, Eleazar Wheelock
   Democrat
   b. Hanover, N. H., April 15, 1782
   d. West Feliciana Parish, La., March 2, 1839
   U. S. Representative, 1835-39

ROBERTSON, Edward White
   Democrat
   b. near Nashville, Tenn., June 13, 1823
   d. Baton Rouge, La., August 2, 1887
   U. S. Representative, 1877-83, 1887

ROBERTSON, Samuel Matthews
　　Democrat
　　b. Plaquemine, La., January 1, 1852
　　d. Baton Rouge, La., December 24, 1911
　　U. S. Representative, 1887-1907

ROBERTSON, Thomas Bolling
　　Democrat
　　b. "Bellefield," near Petersburg, Va., February
　　　　27, 1779
　　d. White Sulphur Springs, Va. (now W. Va.),
　　　　October 5, 1828
　　U. S. Representative, 1812-18
　　Governor of Louisiana, 1820-22

ROMAN, Andre B.
　　National Republican
　　b. St. Landry Parish, La., March 5, 1795
　　d. January 28, 1866
　　Governor of Louisiana, 1831-35, 1839-43 (Whig)

ST. MARTIN, Louis
　　Democrat
　　b. St. Charles Parish, La., May 17, 1820
　　d. New Orleans, La., February 9, 1893
　　U. S. Representative, 1851-53, 1885-87

SANDERS, Jared Young
　　b. near Morgan City, La., January 29, 1869
　　d. Baton Rouge, La., March 23, 1944
　　Governor of Louisiana, 1908-12
　　U. S. Representative, 1917-21

SANDERS, Jared Young, Jr.
　　Democrat
　　b. Franklin, La., April 20, 1892
　　d. Baton Rouge, La., November 29, 1960
　　U. S. Representative, 1934-37, 1941-43

SANDIDGE, John Milton
　　b. near Carnesville, Ga., January 7, 1817
　　d. Bastrop, La., March 30, 1890
　　U. S. Representative, 1855-59

SANDLIN, John Nicholas
　　Democrat
　　b. near Minden, La., February 24, 1872
　　d. Minden, La., December 25, 1957
　　U. S. Representative, 1921-37

SHELDON, Lionel Allen
　　Republican
　　b. Worcester, N.Y., August 30, 1828

d. Pasadena, Calif., January 17, 1917
U. S. Representative, 1869-75
Governor of Territory of New Mexico, 1881-83

SHEPLEY, G. F.
b. Saco, Maine, January 1, 1819
d. July 20, 1878
Military Governor of Louisiana, 1862-64

SHERIDAN, George Augustus
Liberal
b. Millbury, Mass., February 22, 1840
d. National Soldiers' Home, Va., October 7,
        1896
U. S. Representative, 1873-75

SIMPSON, Oramel H.
Democrat
Governor of Louisiana, 1926-28

SLIDELL, John
State Rights Democrat
b. New York, N. Y., 1793
d. Cowes, Isle of Wight, England, July 20,
        1871
U. S. Representative, 1843-45
U. S. Senator, 1853-61

SMITH, George Luke
Republican
b. New Boston, N. H., December 11, 1837
d. Hot Springs, Ark., July 9, 1884
U. S. Representative, 1873-75

SOULE, Pierre
State Rights Democrat
b. Castillon, near Bordeaux, France, August 28,
        1801
d. New Orleans, La., March 26, 1870
U. S. Senator, 1847, 1849-53

SPEARING, James Zacharie
Democrat
b. Alto, Tex., April 23, 1864
d. New Orleans, La., November 2, 1942
U. S. Representative, 1924-31

SPENCER, William Brainerd
Democrat
b. "Home Plantation" in Catahoula Parish, La.,
        February 5, 1835
d. Jalapa, Mexico, February 12, 1882
U. S. Representative, 1876-77

SYPHER, Jacob Hale
    Reoublican
    b. near Millerstown, Pa., June 22, 1837
    d. Baltimore, Md., May 9, 1905
    U. S. Representative, 1868-69, 1870-75

TAYLOR, Miles
    Democrat
    b. Saratoga Springs, N. Y., July 16, 1805
    d. Saratoga Springs, N. Y., September 23, 1873
    U. S. Representative, 1855-61

THIBODEAUX, Bannon Goforth
    b. St. Bridget plantation, near Thibodeaux, La.,
        December 22, 1812
    d. Terrebonne Parish, La., March 5, 1866
    U. S. Representative, 1845-49

THIBODEAUX, Henry S.
    Jefferson Republican
    Governor of Louisiana, 1824

THOMAS, Philemon
    Democrat
    b. Orange County, La., February 9, 1763
    d. Baton Rouge, La., November 18, 1847
    U. S. Representative, 1831-35

THOMPSON, Theo Ashton
    Democrat
    b. Ville Platte, La., March 31, 1916
    d. in an automobile accident in Gastonia, N. C.,
        July 1, 1965
    U. S. Representative, 1953-65

THORNTON, John Randolph
    Democrat
    b. Notoway plantation, near Bayou Goula, La.,
        August 25, 1846
    d. Alexandria, La., December 28, 1917
    U. S. Senator, 1910-15

VIDAL, Michel
    Republican
    b. Chestertown, Md., October 1, 1824
    d. ----
    U. S. Representative, 1868-69

VILLERE, Jacques
    Jefferson Republican
    b. St. John the Baptist Parish, La., April 28,
        1761
    d. March 7, 1830

Governor of Louisiana, 1816-20

WAGGAMAN, George Augustus
    National Republican
    b. "Fairview," near Cambridge, Md., 1790
    d. New Orleans, La., March 22, 1843
    U. S. Senator, 1831-35

WAGGONNER, Joe D., Jr.
    Democrat
    b. near Plain Dealing, La., September 7, 1918
    U. S. Representative, 1961-

WALKER, Joseph
    Democrat
    Governor of Louisiana, 1850-53

WALLACE, Nathaniel Dick
    Democrat
    b. Columbia, Tenn., October 27, 1845
    d. Kenilworth, near Asheville, N. C., July 16,
        1894
    U. S. Representative, 1886-87

WARMOTH, Henry C.
    Republican
    b. McLeansboro, Ill., May 7, 1842
    d. September 30, 1932
    Governor of Louisiana, 1868-72

WATKINS, John Thomas
    Democrat
    b. Minden, La., January 15, 1854
    d. Washington, D. C., April 25, 1925
    U. S. Representative, 1905-21

WELLS, J. Madison
    Conservative Democrat
    b. near Alexandria, La., January 8, 1808
    d. February 28, 1899
    Governor of Louisiana, 1865-67

WEST, Joseph Rodman
    Republican
    b. New Orleans, La., September 19, 1822
    d. Washington, D. C., October 31, 1898
    U. S. Senator, 1871-77

WHITE, Edward Douglass
    Whig
    b. Nashville, Tenn., March 1795
    d. New Orleans, La., April 18, 1847
    U. S. Representative, 1829-34

Governor of Louisiana, 1835-39
U. S. Representative, 1839-43

WHITE, Edward Douglass
    Democrat
    b. near Thibodaux, La., November 3, 1845
    d. Washington, D. C., May 19, 1921
    U. S. Senator, 1891-94
    Associate Justice of the U. S. Supreme Court,
        1894-10
    Chief Justice of the U. S. Supreme Court,
        1910-21

WICKLIFFE, Robert C.
    Democrat
    b. Bardstown, Ky., January 6, 1819
    d. April 18, 1895
    Governor of Louisiana, 1856-60

WICKLIFFE, Robert Charles
    Democrat
    b. Bardstown, Ky., May 1, 1874
    d. Washington, D. C., June 11, 1912
    U. S. Representative, 1909-12

WILKINSON, Theodore Stark
    Democrat
    b. Point Celeste Plantation in Plaquemine
        Parish, near New Orleans, La., December
        18, 1847
    d. New Orleans, La., February 1, 1921
    U. S. Representative, 1887-91

WILLIS, Edwin Edward
    Democrat
    b. Arnaudville, La., October 2, 1904
    U. S. Representative, 1949-69

WILSON, Riley Joseph
    Democrat
    b. near Goldonna, La., November 12, 1871
    d. Ruston, La., February 23, 1946
    U. S. Representative, 1913-37

WILTZ, Louis A.
    Democrat
    b. New Orleans, La., October 22, 1843
    d. October 16, 1881
    Governor of Louisiana, 1880-81

YOUNG, John Smith
    Democrat
    b. near Raleigh, N. C., November 4, 1834

d. Shreveport, La., October 11, 1916
U. S. Representative, 1878-79

PROMINENT PERSONALITIES

The following select list of prominent persons of Louisiana has been selected to indicate the valuable contributions they have made to American life.

BEAUREGARD, Pierre G. T.
    b. St. Bernard Parish, La., May 28, 1815
    d. February 20, 1893
    Army officer
    Graduate U. S. Military Academy, West Point,
        1838
    Served U. S. Army through Mexican War
    Superintendent U. S. Military Academy, West
        Point, 1861
    Resigned from U. S. Army to enter Confederate
        Army, 1861
    Served Confederate Army, 1861-65
    Bombarded Fort Sumter, 1861
    Commissioner of Public Works, New Orleans,
        1888-93

GOTTSCHALK, Louis Moreau
    b. New Orleans, La., May 8, 1829
    d. December 18, 1869
    Pianist and composer
    Made piano debut at Salle Pleyel, Paris,
        France, April 1845
    Compositions: "Tremolo Etude"
                "Bamboula"
                "Last Hope"
    Composed two operas and two symphonies

MCDONOGH, John
    b. Baltimore, Md., December 29, 1779
    d. October 26, 1850
    Went to New Orleans, La. on business, 1800
    Director, Louisiana State Bank, 1806
    Planned to use his money to emancipate his
        slaves and educate the youth of New Orleans
        and Baltimore

NICHOLLS, Francis Tillou
    b. Donaldsonville, La., August 20, 1834
    d. 1912
    Governor of Louisiana, 1877-80, 1888-92
    Chief Justice, Supreme Court of Louisiana, 1893-
        1904

POLK, Leonidas K.
    b. Raleigh, N. C., April 10, 1806

d. June 14, 1864
Graduate U. S. Military Academy, West Point,
    1827
Resigned commission to study theology
Appointed Protestant Episcopal Missionary
    Bishop of the southwest, 1838
Appointed Bishop of Louisiana, 1841
One of founders of the University of the
    South, 1860
Entered Confederate Army as Major General,
    1861

POYDRAS, Julian
    b. France, April 3, 1746
    d. June 14, 1824
    Celebrated French capture of the English fort
        at Baton Rouge with first epic poem in
        Louisiana literature, La Prise du Morne
        du Baton Rouge
    Left liberal sums to Poydras Female Orphan
        Asylum and the Charity Hospital, New
        Orleans, La.

ST. DENIS, Louis Juchereau de
    b. September 17, 1676
    d. June 11, 1744
    Explorer, trader
    Sent by Governor Cadillac to explore possi-
        bilities of trade with Spanish settlements
        in Texas, 1713
    Founded trading post at Natchitockes, 1714

SHREVE, Henry Miller
    b. Burlington County, N. J., October 21, 1785
    d. March 6, 1831
    Steamboat captain
    Owned interest in one of first steamboats on
        Mississippi River, Enterprise, 1814
    Established practicability of steam navigation
        on Mississippi and Ohio Rivers with
        steamboat, Washington, 1816-17
    Shreveport, La. named for him

SIEUR DE BIENVILLE, Jean Baptiste Le Moyne
    b. Montreal, Canada, February 23, 1680
    d. March 7, 1767
    Royal Governor of Louisiana, 1701-12
    Governor for Company of the West, 1718-24
    Royal Governor of Louisiana, 1733-43
    Founded New Orleans, 1718

FIRST STATE CONSTITUTION

CONSTITUTION OF LOUISIANA—1812

We, the Representatives of the People of all that part of the Territory or country ceded under the name of Louisiana, by the treaty made at Paris, on the 30th day of April 1803, between the United States and France, contained in the following limits, to wit: beginning at the mouth of the river Sabine, thence by a line to be drawn along the middle of said river, including all its islands, to the thirty second degree of latitude—thence due north to the Northernmost part of the thirty third degree of north latitude—thence along the said parallel of latitude to the river Mississippi—thence down the said river to the river Iberville, and from thence along the middle of the said river and lakes Maurepas and Pontchartrain to the Gulf of Mexico—thence bounded by the said Gulf to the place of beginning, including all Islands within three leagues of the coast—in Convention Assembled by virtue of an act of Congress, entitled " an act to enable the people of the Territory of Orleans to form a constitution and State government and for the admission of said State into the Union on an equal footing with the original States, and for other purpose; " In order to secure to all the citizens thereof the enjoyment of *the right of life, liberty and property*, do ordain and establish the following constitution or form of government, and do mutually agree with each other to form ourselves into a free and independent State, by the name of the State of Louisiana.

Article 1st

CONCERNING THE DISTRIBUTION OF THE POWERS OF GOVERNMENT.

Sect. 1st. The powers of the government of the State of Louisiana shall be divided into three distinct departments, and each of them be confided to a separate body of Magistracy viz—those which are Legislative to one, those which are executive to another, and those which are judiciary to another.

Sect. 2d. No person or Collection of persons, being one of those departments, shall exercise any power properly belonging to either of the others: except in the instances hereinafter expressly directed or permitted.

Article II

CONCERNING THE LEGISLATIVE DEPARTMENT

Sect. 1st. The Legislative power of this State shall be vested in two distinct branches, the one to be styled the House of Representatives, the other the senate, and both together, the General Assembly of the State of Louisiana.

Sect. 2d. The Members of the House of Representatives shall continue in service for the term of two years from the day of the commencement of the general election.

Sect. 3d. Representatives shall be chosen on the first Monday in July every two years, and the General Assembly shall convene on the first Monday in January in every year, unless a different day be appointed by law, and their sessions shall be held at the Seat of Government.

Sect. 4th. No person shall be a Representative who, at the time of his election is not a free white male citizen of the United States, and hath not attained to the age of twenty one years, and resided in the state two years next preceding his election, and the last year thereof

in the county for which he may be chosen or in the district for which
he is elected in case the said counties may be divided into separate
districts of election, and has not held for one year in the said county
or district landed property to the value of five hundred dollars agreeably to the last list.

SECT. 5th. Elections for Representatives for the several counties
entitled to representation, shall be held at the places of holding their
respecting courts, or in the several election precincts, into which the
Legislature may think proper, from time to time, to divide any or
all of those counties.

SECT. 6th. Representation shall be equal and uniform in this state,
and shall be forever regulated and ascertained by the number of
qualified electors therein. In the year one thousand eight hundred
and thirteen and every fourth year thereafter, an enumeration of all
the electors shall be made in such manner as shall be directed by law.
The number of Representatives shall, in the several years of making
these enumerations be so fixed as not to be less than twenty five nor
more than fifty.

SECT. 7th. The House of Representatives shall choose its speaker
and other officers.

SECT. 8th. In all elections for Representatives every free white male
citizen of the United States, who at the time being, hath attained to
the age of twenty one years and resided in the county in which he
offers to vote one year not preceding the election, and who in the
last six months prior to the said election, shall have paid a state tax,
shall enjoy the right of an elector: provided however that every free
white male citizen of the United States who shall have purchased
land from the United States, shall have the right of voting whenever he shall have the other qualifications of age and residence above
prescribed—Electors shall in all cases, except treason, felony, breach
or surety of peace, be privileged from arrest during their attendance
at, going to or returning from elections.

SECT. 9th. The members of the Senate shall be chosen for the term
of four years, and when assembled shall have the power to choose its
officers annually.

SECT. 10th. The State shall be divided in fourteen senatorial districts, which shall forever remain indivisible, as follows; the Parish
of St. Bernard and Plaquemine including the country above as far as
the land (Des Pécheurs) on the east of the Mississippi and on the
west as far as Bernoudy's canal shall form one district. The city
of New-Orleans beginning at the Nuns' Plantation above and extend-
ing below as far as the above mentioned canal (Des Pécheurs) including the inhabitants of the Bayou St. John, shall form the second
district, the remainder of the county of Orleans shall form the third
district. The counties of German Coast, Acadia, Lafourche, Iberville,
Point Coupée, Concordia, Attakapas, Opelousas, Rapides, Natchitoches and Ouachitta, shall each form one district, and each district
shall elect a Senator.

SECT. 11th. At the Session of the General Assembly after this constitution takes effect, the Senators shall be divided by lot, as equally
as may be, into two classes; the seats of the Senators of the first class
shall be vacated at the expiration of the second year, of the second
class at the expiration of the fourth year: so that one half shall be
chosen every two years, and a rotation thereby kept up perpetually.

SECT. 12th. No person shall be a Senator who, at the time of his election, is not a citizen of the United States, and who hath not attained to the age of twenty seven years; resided in this state four years next preceding his election, and one year in the district, in which he may be chosen; and unless he holds within the same a landed property to the value of one thousand dollars agreeably to the tax list.

SECT. 13th. The first election for Senators shall be general throughout the state, and at the same time that the general election for Representatives is held; and thereafter there shall be a biennial election of Senators to fill the places of those whose time of service may have expired.

SECT. 14th. Not less than a majority of the members of each house of the general assembly, shall form a quorum to do business; but a smaller number may adjourn from day to day, and shall be authorized by law to compel the attendance of absent members, in such manner, and under such penalties as may be prescribed thereby.

SECT. 15th. Each house of the general assembly shall judge of the qualifications, elections and returns of its members, but a contested election shall be determined in such manner as shall be directed by law.

SECT. 16th. Each house of the general assembly may determine the rules of its proceedings, punish a member for disorderly behaviour, and with the concurrence of two thirds, expel a member, but not a second time for the same offence.

SECT. 17th. Each house of the general assembly shall keep and publish weekly a Journal of its proceedings, and the yeas and nays of the members on any question, shall, at the desire of any two of them, be entered on their Journal.

SECT. 18th. Neither house, during the session of the general assembly, shall without the consent of the other, adjourn for more than three days, nor to any other place than that in which they may be sitting.

SECT. 19th. The members of the general assembly shall severally receive from the Public Treasury a compensation for their services, which shall be four dollars per day, during their attendance on, going to and returning from the sessions of their respective houses; Provided that the same may be increased or diminished by law; but no alteration shall take effect during the period of service of the members of the house of Representatives, by whom such alteration shall have been made.

SECT. 20. The members of the general assembly shall in all cases except treason, felony, breach or surety of the peace, be privileged from arrest, during their attendance at the sessions of their respective houses, and in going to or returning from the same, and for any speech or debate in either house, they shall not be questioned in any other place.

SECT. 21. No Senator or Representative shall, during the term for which he was elected, nor for one year thereafter, be appointed or elected to any civil office of profit under this State, which shall have been created, or the emoluments of which shall have been encreased during the time such Senator or Representative was in office, except to such offices or appointments as may be filled by the elections of the people.

Sect. 22. No person while he continues to exercise the functions of a clergyman, priest or teacher of any religious persuasion, society or sect, shall be eligible to the general assembly, or to any office of profit or trust under this State.

Sect. 23. No person who at any time may have been a collector of taxes for the State, or the assistant or deputy of such collector shall be eligible to the general assembly, until he shall have obtained a quietus for the amount of such collection, and for all public moneys for which he may be responsible.

Sect. 24. No bill shall have the force of a law until, on three several days, it be read over in each house of the general assembly, and free discussion allowed thereon; unless in case of urgency, four-fifths of the house where the bill shall be depending, may deem it expedient to dispense with this rule.

Sect. 25. All bills for raising revenue shall originate in the House of Representatives, but the Senate may propose amendments as in other bills; Provided that they shall not introduce any new matter under the colour of an amendment which does not relate to raising a revenue.

Sect. 26. The general assembly shall regulate, by law, by whom and in what manner writs of election shall be issued to fill the vacancies which may happen in either branch thereof.

Article III

CONCERNING THE EXECUTIVE DEPARTMENT

Sect. 1. The supreme executive power of the State shall be vested in a chief magistrate, who shall be styled the Governor of the State of Louisiana.

Sect. 2. The Governor shall be elected for the term of four years in the following manner, the citizens entitled to vote for representatives shall vote for a Governor at the time and place of voting for Representatives and Senators. Their votes shall be returned by the persons presiding over the elections to the seat of government addressed to the president of the Senate, and on the second day of the general assembly, the members of the two houses shall meet in the House of Representatives, and immediately after the two candidates who shall have obtained the greatest number of votes, shall be ballotted for and the one having a majority of votes shall be governor.—Provided however that if more than two candidates have obtained the highest number of votes, it shall be the duty of the general assembly to ballot for them in the manner above prescribed, and in case several candidates should obtain an equal number of votes next to the candidate who has obtained the highest number, it shall be the duty of the general assembly to select in the same manner the candidate who is to be balloted for with him who has obtained the highest number of votes.

Sect. 3. The governor shall be ineligible for the succeeding four years after the expiration of the time for which he shall have been elected.

Sect. 4. He shall be at least thirty five years of age, and a citizen of the United States, and have been an inhabitant of this state at least six years preceding his election, and shall hold in his own right a landed estate of five thousand dollars value, agreeably to the tax list.

SECT. 5. He shall commence the execution of his office on the fourth Monday succeeding the day of his election, and shall continue in the execution thereof, until the end of four weeks next succeeding the election of his successor, and until his successor shall have taken the oaths or affirmations prescribed by this Constitution.

SECT. 6. No member of Congress, or person holding any office under the United States, or minister of any religious society, shall be eligible to the office of Governor.

SECT. 7. The governor shall at stated times, receive for his services a compensation which shall neither be encreased nor diminished during the term for which he shall have been elected.

SECT. 8. He shall be commander in chief of the army and navy of this State, and of the militia thereof except when they shall be called into the service of the United States, but he shall not command personally in the field, unless he shall be advised so to do by a resolution of the general assembly.

SECT. 9th He shall nominate and appoint with the advice and consent of the Senate, Judges, Sheriffs and all other Officers whose offices are established by this Constitution, and whose appointments are not herein otherwise provided for.—Provided however that the Legislature shall have a right to prescribe the mode, of appointment of all other offices to be established by law.

SECT. 10. The governor shall have power to fill up vacancies that may happen during the recess of the Legislature, by granting commissions which shall expire at the end of the next session.

SECT. 11. He shall have power to remit fines and forfeitures, and, except in cases of impeachment, to grant reprieves & pardons, with the approbation of the Senate. In cases of treason he shall have power to grant reprieves until the end of the next session of the general assembly in which the power of pardoning shall be vested.

SECT. 12. He may require information in writing from the officers in the executive department, upon any subject relating to the duties of their respective offices.

SECT. 13. He shall from time to time give to the general assembly information respecting the situation of the state, and recommend to their consideration such measures as he may deem expedient.

SECT. 14. He may on extraordinary occasions convene the general assembly at the seat of government, or at a different place if that should have become dangerous from an enemy or from contagious disorders; and in case of desagreement between the two houses with respect to the time of adjournment, he may ajourn them to such time as he may think proper, not exceeding four months.

SECT. 15. He shall take care that the laws be faithfully executed.

SECT. 16. It shall be his duty to visit the different counties at least once in every two years, to inform himself of the state of the militia and the general condition of the country.

SECT. 17. In case of the impeachment of the governor, his removal from office, death, refusal to qualify, resignation, or absence from the state, the president of the senate shall exercise all the power and authority appertaining to the office of governor, untill another be duly qualified, or the governor absent or impeached shall return or be acquitted.

SECT. 18. The president of the Senate, during the time he administers the government shall receive the same compensation which the governor would have received had he been employed in the duties of his office.

SECT. 19. A secretary of state shall be appointed and commissioned during that term for which the governor shall have been elected, if he shall so long behave himself well, he shall keep a fair register, and attest all official acts and proceedings of the governor, and shall when required, lay the same and all papers, minutes and vouchers relative thereto, before either house of the general assembly, and shall perform such other duties as may be enjoined him by law.

SECT. 20. Every bill which shall have passed both houses shall be presented to the governor, if he approve, he shall sign it, if not he shall return it with his objection to the house in which it shall have originated, who shall enter the objections at large upon their Journal, and proceed to reconsider it—if after such reconsideration, two thirds of all the members elected to that house, shall agree to pass the bill, it shall be sent, with the objections, to the other house, by which it shall likewise be reconsidered and if approved by two thirds of all the members elected to that house, it shall be a law; but in such cases, the votes of both houses shall be determined by yeas and nays, and the names of the members voting for and against the bill, shall be entered on the journal of each house respectively: if any bill shall not be returned by the governor within ten days (Sundays excepted) after it shall have been presented to him, it shall be a law in like manner as if he had signed it, unless the general assembly by their adjournment prevent its return, in which case it shall be a law, unless sent back within three days after their next meeting.

SECT. 21. Every order, resolution or vote, to which the concurrence of both houses may be necessary, except on a question of adjournment, shall be presented to the governor, and before it shall take effect be approved by him; or being disapproved shall be repassed by two thirds of both houses.

SECT. 22. The free white men of this State, shall be armed and disciplined for its defence: but those who belong to religious societies, whose tenets forbid them to carry arms, shall not be compelled so to do, but shall pay an equivalent for personal service.

SECT. 23. The militia of this state shall be organized in such manner as may be hereafter deemed most expedient by the legislature.

ARTICLE IV

CONCERNING THE JUDICIARY DEPARTMENT

SECT. 1st. The judiciary power shall be vested in a supreme court and inferior courts.

SECT. 2d. The supreme court shall have appellate jurisdiction only, which jurisdiction shall extend to all civil cases when the matter in dispute shall exceed the sum of three hundred dollars.

SECT. 3d. The supreme court shall consist of not less than three judges, nor more than five: the majority of whom shall form a quorum; each of the said judges shall receive a salary of five thousand dollars annually. The supreme court shall hold its sessions at the places hereinafter mentioned; and for that purpose the state is hereby divided into two districts of appellate jurisdiction, in each of which the supreme court shall administer justice in the manner hereafter prescribed. The Eastern district to consist of the counties of New Orleans, German Coast, Acadia, Lafourche, Iberville, and Point Coupee; the western district to consist of the counties of Attakapas, Opelousas, Rapides, Concordia, Natchitoches, and Ouachita. The supreme court shall hold its sessions in each year, for the Eastern district in New-Orleans during the months of November, December, January, February, March, April, May, June, and July; and for the western district, at Opelousas during the months of August, September and October: for five years: Provided however, That every five years the legislature may change the place of holding said court in the western district. The said court shall appoint its own clerks.

SECT. 4th. The legislature is authorised to establish such inferior courts as may be convenient to the administration of justice.

SECT. 5th. The judges both of the supreme and inferior courts shall hold their offices during good behaviour; but for any reasonable cause which shall not be sufficient ground for impeachment, the Governor shall remove any of them, on the address of three fourths of each house of the general assembly: Provided however, That the cause or causes for which such removal may be required, shall be stated at length in the address, and inserted on the journal of each house.

SECT. 6th. The judges, by virtue of their office, shall be conservators of the peace throughout the state; the style of all process shall be " The State of Louisiana." All prosecutions shall be carried on in the name and by the authority of the state of Louisiana, and conclude " against the peace and dignity of the same."

SECT. 7. There shall be an attorney general for the state, and as many other prosecuting attorneys for the state as may be hereafter found necessary. The said attorneys shall be appointed by the Governor with the advice and approbation of the Senate. Their duties shall be determined by law.

SECT. 8. All commissions shall be in the name, and by the authority of, the state of Louisiana, and sealed with the state seal, and signed by the Governor.

SECT. 9. The state treasurer, and printer or printers of the state, shall be appointed, annually, by the joint vote of both houses of the general assembly: Provided, That during the recess of the same, the Governor shall have power to fill vacancies which may happen in either of the said offices.

SECT. 10. The clerks of the several courts shall be removable for breach of good behaviour, by the court of appeals only, who shall be judge of the fact, as well as of the law.

SECT 11. The existing laws in this territory, when this constitution goes into effect, shall continue to be in force until altered or abolished by the Legislature: Provided however, that the Legislature shall never adopt any system or code of laws, by a general reference to the said system or code, but in all cases, shall specify the several provisions of the laws it may enact.

SECT 12. The judges of all courts within this state, shall, as often as it may be possible so to do, in every definitive judgment, refer to the particular law, in virtue of which such judgment may have been rendered. and in all cases adduce the reasons on which their judgment is founded.

ARTICLE V

CONCERNING IMPEACHMENT.

SECT. 1. The power of impeachment shall be vested in the House of Representatives alone.

SECT. 2. All impeachments shall be tried by the Senate when sitting for that purpose, the senators shall be upon oath or affirmation, and no person shall be convicted without the concurrence of two thirds of the members present.

SECT. 3. The governor and all the civil officers, shall be liable to impeachment for any misdemeanor in office, but judgment, in such cases, shall not extend further than to removal from office and disqualification to hold any office of honor trust or profit under this State; but the parties convicted shall nevertheless, be liable and subject to indictment, trial and punishment according to law.

ARTICLE VI

GENERAL PROVISIONS

SECT. 1. Members of the general assembly and all officers executive and judicial. before they enter upon the execution of their respective offices. shall take the following oath or affirmation: " I (A. B.) do solemnly swear (or affirm) that I will faithfully and impartially discharge and perform all the duties incumbent on me as—according to the best of my abilities and understanding, agreeably to the rules and regulations of the Constitution, and the laws of this State; so help me God! "

SECT. 2. Treason against the State. shall consist only in levying war against it or in adhering to its enemies. giving them aid and comfort. No person shall be convicted of treason. unless on the testimony of two witnesses to the same overt act, or his own confession in open court.

SECT. 3. Every person shall be disqualified from serving as governor. Senator or Representative for the term for which he shall have been elected. who shall have been convicted of having given or offered any bribe to procure his election.

SECT. 4. Laws shall be made to exclude from office and from suffrage those who shall thereafter be convicted of bribery. perjury, forgery or other high crimes or misdemeanors. the privilege of free suffrage shall be supported by laws regulating elections and prohibiting under adequate penalties. all undue influence thereon, from power, bribery. tumult. or other improper practices.

SECT. 5. No money shall be drawn from the treasury, but in pursuance of appropriations made by law: nor shall any appropriation of money for the support of an army be made for a longer term than one year: and a regular statement and account of the receipts and expenditures of all public moneys. shall be published annually.

SECT. 6. It shall be the duty of the general assembly to pass such laws as may be necessary and proper to decide differences by arbitrators, to be appointed by the parties, who may choose that summary mode of adjustment.

SECT. 7. All civil officers for the state at large shall reside within the State, and all district or county officers within their respective districts or counties, and shall keep their respective offices at such places therein as may be required by law.

SECT. 8. The Legislature shall determine the time of duration of the several public offices when such time shall not have been fixed by this Constitution, and all civil officers except the governor and judges of the superior and inferior courts shall be removable by an address of two thirds of the members of both houses, except those, the removal of whom has been otherwise provided for by this Constitution.

SECT. 9. Absence on the business of this State or of the United States, shall not forfeit a residence once obtained, so as to deprive any one of the rights of suffrage, or of being elected or appointed to any office under this State, under the exceptions contained in this Constitution.

SECT. 10. It shall be the duty of the general assembly to regulate by law in what cases, and what deduction from the salaries of public officers shall be made for neglect of duty in their official capacity.

SECT. 11. Returns of all elections for the members of the general assembly, shall be made to the secretary of state for the time being.

SECT. 12. The Legislature shall point out the manner in which a man coming into the country shall declare his residence.

SECT. 13. In all elections by the people, and also by the Senate and House of Representatives jointly or separately, the vote shall be given by ballot.

SECT. 14. No members of Congress, nor person holding or exercising any office of trust or profit under the United States, or either of them, or under any foreign powers shall be eligible as a member of the general assembly of this State, or hold or exercise any office of trust or profit under the same.

SECT. 15. All laws that may be passed by the Legislature, and the public records of this State, and the judicial and legislative written proceedings of the same, shall be promulgated, preserved and conducted in the language in which the constitution of the United States is written.

SECT. 16. The general assembly shall direct by law how persons who are now or may hereafter become securities for public officers, may be relieved or discharged on account of such securityship.

SCET. 17. No power of suspending the laws of this State shall be exercised, unless by the Legislature, or its authority.

SECT. 18. In all criminal prosecutions, the accused have the right of being heard by himself or counsel, of demanding the nature and cause of the accusation against him, of meeting the witnesses face to face, of having compulsory process for obtaining witnesses in his favour, and prosecutions by indictment or information, a speedy public trial by an impartial jury of the vicinage, nor shall he be compelled to give evidence against himself.

SECT. 19. All prisoners shall be bailable by sufficient securities, unless for capital offences, where the proof is evident or presumption great, and the privilege of the writ of Habeas Corpus shall not be suspended unless when in cases of rebellion or invasion the public safety may require it.

SECT. 20. No *ex post facto* law nor any law impairing the obligation of contracts shall be passed.

SECT. 21. Printing presses shall be free to every person who undertakes to examine the proceedings of the Legislature, or any branch of the government, and no law shall ever be made to restrain the right thereof. The free communication of thoughts and opinions is one of the invaluable rights of man, and every citizen may freely speak, write and print on any subject, being responsible for the abuse of that liberty.

SECT. 22. Emigration from the State shall not be prohibited.

SECT. 23. The citizens of the town of New-Orleans shall have the right of appointing the several public officers necessary for the administration and the police of the said city, pursuant to the mode of election which shall be prescribed by the Legislature: Provided that the mayor and recorder be ineligible to a seat in the general assembly.

SECT. 24. The seat of government shall continue at New Orleans until removed by law.

SECT. 25. All laws contrary to this Constitution shall be null and void.

ARTICLE VII

MODE OF REVISING THE CONSTITUTION

SECT. 1. When experience shall point out the necessity of amending this Constitution, and a majority of all the members elected to each house of the general assembly, shall, within the first twenty days of their stated annual session, concur in passing a law, specifying the alterations intended to be made, for taking the sense of the good people of this state, as to the necessity and expediency of calling a convention, it shall be the duty of the several returning officers, at the next general election which shall be held for Representatives after the passage of such law, to open a poll for, and make return to the secretary for the time being, of the names of all those entitled to vote for Representatives, who have voted for calling a convention; and if thereupon, it shall appear that a majority of all the citizens of this state, entitled to vote for Representatives, have voted for a convention, the general assembly, shall direct that a similar poll shall be opened, and taken for the next year; and if thereupon, it shall appear that a majority of all the citizens of this state entitled to vote for Representatives, have voted for a convention, the general assembly shall, at their next session, call a convention to consist of as many members as there shall be in the general assembly, and no more, to be chosen in same manner and proportion, at the same places and at the same time, that Representatives are, by citizens entitled to vote for Representatives: and to meet within three months after the said election, for the purpose of re-adopting, amending or changing this constitution. But if it shall appear by the vote of either year, as aforesaid, that a majority of all the citizens entitled to vote for Representatives, did not vote for a convention, a convention shall not be called.

SCHEDULE.

SECT. 1. That no inconveniences may arise from the change of a territorial to permanent state government, it is declared by the Convention that all rights, suits, actions, prosecutions, claims and contracts, both as it respects individuals and bodies corporate, shall continue as if no change had taken place in this government in virtue of the laws now in force.

SECT. 2. All fines, penalties and forfeitures, due and owing to the territory of Orleans shall inure to the use of the state. All bonds executed to the governor or any other officer in his official capacity in the territory, shall pass over to the governor or to the officers of the State and their successors in office, for the use of the State, by him or by them to be respectively assigned over to the use of those concerned, as the case may be.

SECT. 3. The governor, secretary and judges, and all other officers under the territorial government, shall continue in the exercise of their duties of their respective departments until the said officers are superceded under the authority of this Constitution.

SECT. 4. All laws now in force in this territory, not inconsistent with this constitution, shall continue and remain in full effect until repealed by the legislature.

SECT. 5. The governor of this state shall make use of his private seal, until a state seal be procured.

SECT. 6. The oaths of office herein directed to be taken, may be administered by any justice of the peace, until the legislature shall otherwise direct.

SECT. 7. At the expiration of the time after which this constitution is to go into operation, or immediately after official information shall have been received that congress have approved of the same, the president of the Convention shall issue writs of election to the proper officers in the different counties, enjoining them to cause an election to be held for governor and members of the general assembly, in each of their respective districts. The election shall commence on the fourth Monday following the day of the date of the President's proclamation, and shall take place on the same day throughout the state. The mode and duration of the said election shall be determined by the laws now in force: Provided however, that in case of absence or disability of the President of the Convention, to cause the said election to be carried into effect, the Secretary of the Convention shall discharge the duties hereby imposed on the President, and that in case of absence of the secretary a committee of Messrs Blanque, Brown, and Urquhart or a majority of them, shall discharge the duties herein imposed on the secretary of the convention—and the members of the general assembly thus elected shall assemble on the fourth Monday thereafter at the seat of government. The governor and members of the general assembly for this time only, shall enter upon the duties of their respective offices, immediately after their election, and shall continue in office in the same manner and during the same period they would have done had they been elected on the first Monday of July 1812.

SECT. 8. untill the first enumeration shall be made as directed in the sixth section of the second article of this Constitution, the, county of

Orleans shall be entitled to Six Representatives to be elected as follows: one by the first senatorial district within the said county, four by the second district, and one by the third district—The county of German Coast, to two Representatives, the county of Acadia, to two Representatives; the county of Iberville, to two Representatives; the county of Lafourche, to two Representatives; to be elected as follows: one by the parish of the assumption, and the other by the parish of the interior: the county of Rapides, to two Representatives: the county of Natchitoches, to one Representative; the county of Concordia, to one Representative; the county of Ouachitta, to one Representative; the county of Opelloussas, to two Representatives; the county of Attakapas, to three Representatives to be elected as follows: two by the parish of St. Martin and the third by the parish of St. Mary, and the respective senatorial districts created by this Constitution, to one senator each.

Done in Convention, at New Orleans, the twenty second day of the month of January, in the year of our Lord one thousand eight hundred and twelve, and of the independence of the United States of America, the thirty-sixth.

J. POYDRAS,
President of the Convention.

ELIGIUS FROMENTIN,
Secretary of the Convention.

SELECTED DOCUMENTS

The documents selected for this section have been chosen to illustrate the various attitudes, concerns and issues in the development of Louisiana. Documents relating specifically to the constitutional development of Louisiana will be found in volume four-A of <u>Sources and Documents of United States Constitutions</u>, a companion reference collection to the Columbia University volumes previously cited.

THE IMPORTANCE OF LOUISIANA TO THE STATES

By President Thomas Jefferson

IT IS made plain in the accompanying letters from Jefferson to Robert R. Livingston, American Minister at Paris, and, the second, to M. du Pont de Nemours, a Delaware powder manufacturer with influential French connections, that the retention of Louisiana by France would lead to war with the United States. Both letters were written by our third President, in Washington, April, 1802, shortly after news reached this country that Spain, by a secret treaty, had retroceded Louisiana and the Floridas to France. Also that Spain had withdrawn the right of deposit secured to the inhabitants of the United States by the treaty of 1795, and that the delivery was to be made at an early date.

Jefferson desired and was determined, so far as lay in his power, to keep the United States a self-sustained nation. This, he saw, would be impossible if France possessed the outlet of the Mississippi valley.

THE cession of Louisiana and the Floridas by Spain to France, works most sorely on the United States. On this subject the Secretary of State has written to you fully, yet I cannot forbear recurring to it personally, so deep is the impression it makes on my mind. It completely reverses all the political relations of the United States, and will form a new epoch in our political course. Of all nations of any consideration, France is the one which, hitherto, has offered the fewest points on which we could have any conflict of right, and the most points of a communion of interests. From these causes, we have ever looked to her as our natural friend, as one with which we never could have an

America. Great Crises In Our History Told By Its Makers. Vol. 4. Chicago: Veterans of Foreign Wars Americanization Department, 1925.

occasion of difference. Her growth, therefore, we
viewed as our own, her misfortunes ours. There is
on the globe one single spot, the possessor of which is
our natural and habitual enemy. It is New Orleans,
through which the produce of three-eighths of our territory must pass to market, and from its fertility it
will ere long yield more than half of our whole produce, and contain more than half of our inhabitants.

France, placing herself in that door, assumes to us
the attitude of defiance. Spain might have retained
it quietly for years. Her pacific dispositions, her
feeble state, would induce her to increase our facilities
there, so that her possession of the place would be
hardly felt by us, and it would not, perhaps, be very
long before some circumstance might rise, which
might make the cession of it to us the price of something of more worth to her. Not so can it ever be in
the hands of France: the impetuosity of her temper,
the energy and restlessness of her character, placed in
a point of eternal friction with us, and our character,
which, though quiet and loving peace and the pursuit
of wealth, is high-minded, despising wealth in com-
petition with insult or injury, enterprising and ener-
getic as any nation on earth; these circumstances render it impossible that France and the United States
can continue long friends, when they meet in so irrita-
ble a position. They, as well as we, must be blind if
they do not see this; and we must be very improvident
if we do not begin to make arrangements on that
hypothesis.

The day that France takes possession of New Orleans, fixes the sentence which is to restrain her forever within her low-water mark. It seals the union of two nations, who, in conjunction, can maintain exclusive possession of the ocean. From that moment, we must marry ourselves to the British fleet and nation. We must turn all our attention to a maritime force, for which our resources place us on very high ground; and having formed and connected together a power which may render reinforcement of her settlements here impossible to France, make the first cannon which shall be fired in Europe the signal for the tearing up any settlement she may have made, and for holding the two continents of America in sequestration for the common purposes of the United British and American nations.

This is not a state of things we seek or desire. It is one which this measure, if adopted by France, forces on us as necessarily, as any other cause, by the laws of nature, brings on its necessary effect. It is not from a fear of France that we deprecate this measure proposed by her. For however greater her force is than ours, compared in the abstract, it is nothing in comparison to ours, when to be exerted on our soil. But it is from a sincere love of peace, and a firm persuasion, that bound to France by the interests and the strong sympathies still existing in the minds of our citizens, and holding relative positions which insure their continuance, we are secure of a long course

of peace. Whereas, the change of friends, which will
be rendered necessary if France changes that position,
embarks us necessarily as a belligerent power in the
first war of Europe. In that case, France will have
held possession of New Orleans during the interval
of a peace, long or short, at the end of which it will
be wrested from her. Will this short-lived possession
have been an equivalent to her for the transfer of
such a weight into the scale of her enemy? Will not
the amalgamation of a young, thriving nation, continue to that enemy the health and force which are
at present so evidently on the decline? And will a
few years' possession of New Orleans add equally to
the strength of France?

    She may say she needs Louisiana for the supply of
her West Indies. She does not need it in time of
peace, and in war she could not depend on them,
because they would be so easily intercepted. I should
suppose that all these considerations might, in some
proper form, be brought into view of the government
of France. Though stated by us, it ought not to
give offense; because we do not bring them forward
as a menace, but as consequences not controllable by
us, but inevitable from the course of things. We
mention them, not as things which we desire by any
means, but as things we deprecate; and we beseech a
friend to look forward and to prevent them for our
common interest.

    If France considers Louisiana, however, as indis-
pensable for her views, she might perhaps be willing

to look about for arrangements which might reconcile it to our interests. If anything could do this, it would be the ceding to us the island of New Orleans and the Floridas. This would certainly, in a great degree, remove the causes of jarring and irritation between us, and perhaps for such a length of time, as might produce other means of making the measure permanently conciliatory to our interests and friendships. It would, at any rate, relieve us from the necessity of taking immediate measures for countervailing such an operation by arrangements in another quarter. But still we should consider New Orleans and the Floridas as no equivalent for the risk of a quarrel with France, produced by her vicinage.

I have no doubt you have urged these considerations, on every proper occasion, with the government where you are. They are such as must have effect, if you can find means of producing thorough reflection on them by that government. . . . Every eye in the United States is now fixed on the affairs of Louisiana. Perhaps nothing since the Revolutionary War, has produced more uneasy sensations through the body of the nation. Notwithstanding temporary bickerings have taken place with France, she has still a strong hold on the affections of our citizens generally. I have thought it not amiss, by way of supplement to the letters of the Secretary of State, to write you this private one, to impress you with the importance we affix to this transaction. . . .

I THINK it safe to enclose you my letters for Paris
. . . I leave the letters for Chancellor Livingston
open for your perusal. . . . I wish you to be possessed of the subject, because you may be able to
impress on the government of France the inevitable
consequences of their taking possession of Louisiana;
and though, as I here mention, the cession of New
Orleans and the Floridas to us would be a palliation,
yet I believe it would be no more, and that this measure will cost France, and perhaps not very long hence,
a war which will annihilate her on the ocean, and
place that element under the despotism of two nations, which I am not reconciled to the more because
my own would be one of them. Add to this the exclusive appropriation of both continents of America
as a consequence.

I wish the present order of things to continue, and
with a view to this I value highly a state of friendship
between France and us. You know too well how
sincere I have ever been in these dispositions to doubt
them. You know, too, how much I value peace, and
how unwillingly I should see any event take place
which would render war a necessary resource; and
that all our movements should change their character
and object. I am thus open with you, because I trust
that you will have it in your power to impress on that
government considerations, in the scale against which
the possession of Louisiana is nothing. In Europe,
nothing but Europe is seen, or supposed to have any
right in the affairs of nations; but this little event of

France's possessing herself of Louisiana, which is thrown in as nothing, as a mere make-weight in the general settlement of accounts,—this speck which now appears as an almost invisible point in the horizon, is the embryo of a tornado which will burst on the countries on both sides of the Atlantic, and involve in its effects their highest destinies. That it may yet be avoided is my sincere prayer; and if you can be the means of informing the wisdom of Bonaparte of all its consequences, you have deserved well of both countries. Peace and abstinence from European interferences are our objects, and so will continue while the present order of things in America remain uninterrupted. . . .

THE TERRITORIAL GOVERNMENT OF ORLEANS—1805

[Eighth Congress, Second Session]

An Act further providing for the government of the territory of Orleans

Be it enacted by the Senate and House of Representatives of the United States of America in Congress assembled, That the President of the United States be, and he is herby, authorized to establish within the territory of Orleans a government in all respects similar (except as is herein otherwise provided) to that now exercised in the Mississippi territory; and shall, in the recess of the Senate, but to be nominated at their next meeting, for their advice and consent, appoint all the officers necessary therein, in conformity with the ordinance of Congress, made on the thirteenth day of July, one thousand seven hundred and eighty-seven; and that from and after the establishment of the said government, the inhabitants of the territory of Orleans shall be entitled to and enjoy all the rights, privileges, and advantages secured by the said ordinance, and now enjoyed by the people of the Mississippi territory.

SEC. 2. *And be it further enacted,* That so much of the said ordinance of Congress as relates to the organization of a general assembly, and prescribes the powers thereof, shall, from and after the fourth day of July next, be in force in the said territory of Orleans; and in order to carry the same into operation, the governor of the said territory shall cause to be elected twenty-five representatives, for which purpose he shall lay off the said territory into convenient election-districts, on or before the first Monday of October next, and give due notice thereof throughout the same; and shall appoint the most convenient time and place within each of the said districts, for holding the elections; and shall nominate a proper officer or officers to preside at and conduct the same, and to return to him the names of the persons who may have been duly elected. All subsequent elections shall be regulated by the legislature; and the number of representatives shall be determined, and the apportionment made, in the manner prescribed by the said ordinance.

SEC. 3. *And be it further enacted,* That the representatives to be chosen as aforesaid shall be convened by the governor, in the city of Orleans, on the first Monday in November next; and the first general assembly shall be convened by the governor as soon as may be convenient, at the city of Orleans, after the members of the legislative council shall be appointed and commissioned; and the general assembly shall meet, at least once in every year, and such meeting shall be on the first Monday in December, annually, unless they shall, by law, appoint a different day. Neither house, during the session, shall, without the consent of the other, adjourn for more than three days, nor to any other place than that in which the two branches are sitting.

SEC. 4. *And be it further enacted,* That the laws in force in the said territory at the commencement of this act, and not inconsistent with the provisions thereof, shall continue in force until altered, modified, or repealed by the legislature.

SEC. 5. *And be it further enacted,* That the second paragraph of the said ordinance, which regulates the descent and distribution of estates; and also the sixth article of compact which is annexed to and makes part of said ordinance, are hereby declared not to extend to but are excluded from all operation within the said territory of Orleans.

SEC. 6. *And be it further enacted*, That the governor, secretary, and judges to be appointed by virtue of this act shall be severally allowed the same compensation which is now allowed to the governor, secretary, and judges of the territory of Orleans. And all the additional officers authorized by this act shall respectively receive the same compensation for their services as are by law established for similar offices in the Mississippi territory, to be paid quarter-yearly out of the revenues of impost and tonnage accruing within the said territory of Orleans.

SEC. 7. *And be it further enacted*, That whenever it shall be ascertained by an actual census or enumeration of the inhabitants of the territory of Orleans, taken by proper authority, that the number of free inhabitants included therein shall amount to sixty thousand, they shall thereupon be authorized to form for themselves a constitution and state government, and be admitted into the Union upon the footing of the original states, in all respects whatever, conformably to the provisions of the third article of the treaty concluded at Paris on the thirtieth of April, one thousand eight hundred and three, between the United States and the French Republic: *Provided*, That the constitution so to be established shall be republican, and not inconsistent with the constitution of the United States, nor inconsistent with the ordinance of the late Congress, passed the thirteenth day of July, one thousand seven hundred and eighty-seven, so far as the same is made applicable to the territorial government hereby authorized to be established: *Provided, however*, That Congress shall be at liberty, at any time prior to the admission of the inhabitants of the said territory to the right of a separate state, to alter the boundaries thereof as they may judge proper: *Except only*, That no alteration shall be made which shall procrastinate the period for the admission of the inhabitants thereof to the rights of a state government according to the provision of this act.

SEC. 8. *And be it further enacted*, That so much of an act intituled "An act erecting Louisiana into two territories, and providing for the temporary government thereof," as is repugnant with this act, shall, from and after the first Monday of November next, be repealed. And the residue of the said act shall continue in full force until repealed, anything in the sixteenth section of the said act to the contrary notwithstanding.

Approved, March 2, 1805.

THE TERRITORY OF LOUISIANA—1805 [a]

[EIGHTH CONGRESS, SECOND SESSION.]

An Act further providing for the government of the district of Louisiana.

Be it enacted by the Senate and House of Representatives of the United States of America in Congress assembled, That all that part of the country ceded by France to the United States, under the general name of Louisiana, which, by an act of the last session of Congress, was erected into a separate district, to be called the district of Louisiana, shall henceforth be known and designated by the name and title of the Territory of Louisiana, the government whereof shall be organized and administered as follows: The executive power shall be vested in a governor, who shall reside in said territory, and hold his office during the term of three years, unless sooner removed by the President of the United States. He shall be commander-in-chief of the militia of the said territory, superintendent ex officio of Indian affairs, and shall appoint and commission all officers in the same below the rank of general officers; shall have power to grant pardons for offences against the same, and reprieves for those against the United States until the decision of the President thereon shall be known.

SEC. 2. There shall be a secretary, whose commission shall continue in force for four years, unless sooner revoked by the President of the United States, who shall reside in the said territory, and whose duty it shall be, under the direction of the governor, to record and preserve all the papers and proceedings of the executive and all the acts of the governor and of the legislative body, and transmit authentic copies of the same every six months to the President of the United States. In case of a vacancy of the office of governor, the government of the said territory shall be exercised by the secretary.

SEC. 3. The legislative power shall (be) vested in the governor and in three judges, or a majority of them, who shall have power to establish inferior courts in the said territory, and prescribe their jurisdiction and duties, and to make all laws which they may deem conducive to the good government of the inhabitants thereof: *Provided, however,* That no law shall be valid which is inconsistent with the constitution and laws of the United States, or which shall lay any person under restraint or disability on account of his religious opinions, profession, or worship, in all of which he shall be free to maintain his own and not be burthened with those of another: *And provided also,* That in all criminal prosecutions the trial shall be by a jury of twelve good and lawful men of the vicinage, and in all civil cases of the value of one hundred dollars the trial shall be by jury, if either of the parties require it. And the governor shall publish throughout the said territory all the laws which may be made as aforesaid, and shall, from time to time, report the same to the President of the United States, to be laid before Congress, which, if disapproved of by Congress, shall thenceforth cease and be of no effect.

SEC. 4. There shall be appointed three judges, who shall hold their offices for the term of four years, who, or any two of them, shall hold annually two courts within the said district, at such place as will be most convenient to the inhabitants thereof in general: shall possess the same jurisdiction which is possessed by the judges of the

---

[a] This was originally called the District of Louisiana, but no part of it is included in the present State of Louisiana, which was originally the Territory of Orleans.

Indiana territory, and shall continue in session until all the business depending before them shall be disposed of.

SEC. 5. *And be it further enacted*, That for the more convenient distribution of justice, the prevention of crimes and injuries, and execution of process, criminal and civil, the governor shall proceed, from time to time, as circumstances may require, to lay out those parts of the territory in which the Indian title shall have been extinguished into districts, subject to such alterations as may be found necessary, and he shall appoint thereto such magistrates and other civil officers as he may deem necessary, whose several powers and authorities shall be regulated and defined by law.

SEC. 6. *And be it further enacted*, That the governor, secretary, and judges to be appointed by virtue of this act shall respectively receive the same compensations for their services as are by law established for similar offices in the Indiana territory, to be paid quarter-yearly out of the treasury of the United States.

SEC. 7. *And be it further enacted*, That the governor, secretary, judges, justices of the peace, and all other officers, civil or military, before they enter upon the duties of their respective offices, shall take an oath, or affirmation, to support the constitution of the United States and for the faithful discharge of the duties of their office: the governor before the President of the United States, or before a judge of the supreme or district court of the United States, or before such other person as the President of the United States shall authorize to administer the same: the secretary and judges before the governor; and all other officers before such person as the governor shall direct.

SEC. 8. *And be it further enacted*, That the governor, secretary, and judges, to be appointed by virtue of this act, and all the additional officers authorized thereby, or by the act for erecting Louisiana into two territories, and providing for the temporary government thereof, shall be appointed by the President of the United States in the recess of the Senate, but shall be nominated at their next meeting for their advice and consent.

SEC. 9. *And be it further enacted*, That the laws and regulations in force in the said district at the commencement of this act, and not inconsistent with the provisions thereof, shall continue in force until altered, modified, or repealed by the legislature.

SEC. 10. *And be it further enacted*, That so much of an act intituled "An act erecting Louisiana into two territories, and providing for the temporary government thereof," as is repugnant to this act, shall, from and after the fourth day of July next, be repealed; on which said fourth day of July this act shall commence and have full force.

Approved. March 3, 1805.

Petition for Representative Government (1804)

BY INHABITANTS OF LOUISIANA

This petition was the work of Edward Livingston, who had removed to New Orleans in 1804. It secured a change in the government of the territory, which was the first step toward the incorporation of Louisiana into the Union and the first announcement of the extension of the Constitution over acquired territory. — Bibliography as in No. 113 above.

WE, the subscribers, planters, merchants, and other inhabitants of Louisiana, respectfully approach the Legislature of the United States with a memorial of our rights, a remonstrance against certain laws which contravene them, and a petition for that redress to which the laws of nature, sanctioned by positive stipulation, have entitled us. . . .

Disavowing any language but that of respectful remonstrance, disdaining any other but that which befits a manly assertion of our rights, we pray leave to examine the law for erecting Louisiana into two Territories and providing for the temporary government thereof, to compare its provisions with our rights, and its whole scope with the letter and spirit of the treaty which binds us to the United States.

The first section erects the country south of the thirty-third degree into a Territory of the United States, by the name of the Territory of Orleans.

The second gives us a Governor appointed for three years by the President of the United States.

The fourth vests in him and in a council, also chosen by the President, all Legislative power, subject to the revision of Congress, especially guarding against any interference with public property either by taxation or sale.

And the fifth establishes a Judiciary, to consist of a Supreme Court, having exclusive criminal and original jurisdiction without appeal for all causes above the value of one hundred dollars, and such inferior courts as the Legislature of the Territory may establish. The judges of the superior court are appointed by the President, to continue in office four years.

This is the summary of our constitution ; this is so far the accomplishment of a treaty engagement to "incorporate us into the Union, and admit us to all the rights, advantages, and immunities of American citizens." And this is the promise performed, which was made by our first magistrate in your name, " that you would receive us as brothers,

Albert Bushnell Hart, ed. American History Told by Contemporaries. Vol. III. New York: The Macmillan Company, 1898.

and hasten to extend to us a participation in those invaluable rights which had formed the basis of your unexampled prosperity." . . .

Taxation without representation, an obligation to obey laws without any voice in their formation, the undue influence of the executive upon legislative proceedings, and a dependent judiciary, formed, we believe, very prominent articles in the list of grievances complained of by the United States, at the commencement of their glorious contest for freedom . . .

Are truths, then, so well founded, so universally acknowledged, inapplicable only to us? Do political axioms on the Atlantic become problems when transferred to the shores of the Mississippi? . . . Where, we ask respectfully, where is the circumstance that is to exclude us from a participation in these rights? . . .

. . . To deprive us of our right of election, we have been represented as too ignorant to exercise it with wisdom, and too turbulent to enjoy it with safety.   Sunk in ignorance, effeminated by luxury, debased by oppression, we were, it was said, incapable of appreciating a free constitution, if it were given, or feeling the deprivation, if it were denied.

The sentiments which were excited by this humiliating picture may be imagined, but cannot be expressed, consistent with the respect we owe to your honorable body. . . .

As to the degree of information diffused through the country, we humbly request that some more correct evidence may be produced than the superficial remarks that have been made by travellers or residents, who neither associate with us nor speak our language.   Many of us are native citizens of the United States, who have participated in that kind of knowledge which is there spread among the people ; the others generally are men who will not suffer by a comparison with the population of any other colony. . . .

For our love of order and submission to the laws we can confidently appeal to the whole history of our settlement, and particularly to what has lately passed in those dangerous moments when it was uncertain at what point our political vibrations would stop ; when national prejudice, personal interest, factious views, and ambitious designs, might be supposed to combine for the interruption of our repose ; when, in the frequent changes to which we have been subject, the authority of one nation was weakened before the other had established its power. . . .

But let us admit . . . that there is no clause for us in the great charter of nature, and that we must look for our freedom to another source ; yet we are not without a claim ; one arising from solemn stipulation, and, according to our ideas, full, obligatory, and unequivocal.

The third article of the treaty lately concluded at Paris, declares that "the inhabitants of the ceded territory shall be incorporated into the Union of the United States, and admitted as soon as possible, according to the principles of the Federal Constitution, to the enjoyment of all the rights, advantages, and immunities, of citizens of the United States, and in the mean time they shall be protected in the enjoyment of their liberty, property, and the exercise of the religion they profess.". . .

The inhabitants of the ceded territory are to be "incorporated into the Union of the United States ;" these words can in no sense be satisfied by the act in question. A Territory governed in the manner it directs may be a province of the United States, but can by no construction be said to be incorporated into the Union. To be incorporated into the Union must mean to form a part of it ; but to every component part of the United States the Constitution has guarantied a republican form of Government, and this, as we have already shown, has no one principle of republicanism in its composition ; it is, therefore, not a compliance with the letter of the treaty, and is totally inconsistent with its spirit, which certainly intends some stipulations in our favor. . . .
If any doubt, however, could possibly arise on the first member of the sentence, it must vanish by a consideration of the second, which provides for their admission to the rights, privileges, and immunities, of citizens of the United States. But this Government, as we have shown, is totally incompatible with those rights. Without any vote in the election of our Legislature, without any check upon our Executive, without any one incident of self-government, what valuable "privilege" of citizenship is allowed us, what "right" do we enjoy, of what "immunity" can we boast, except, indeed, the degrading exemption from the cares of legislation, and the burden of public affairs? . . .

We know not with what view the territory north of the thirty-third degree has been severed from us, and carried with it the distinguishing name which belonged to us, and to which we are attached ; the convenience of the inhabitants we humbly apprehend would have been better consulted by preserving the connexion of the whole province until a greater degree of population made a division necessary. If this division should operate so as to prolong our state of political tutelage, on account of any supposed deficiency of numbers, we cannot but consider it as injurious to our rights, and therefore enumerate it among those points of which we have reason to complain. . . .

There is one subject, however, extremely interesting to us, in which great care has been taken to prevent any interference even by the Governor and Council, selected by the President himself. The African trade is absolutely prohibited, and severe penalties imposed on a traffic free to all the Atlantic States who choose to engage in it, and as far as relates to procuring the subjects of it from other States, permitted even in the Territory of the Mississippi.

It is not our intention to enter into arguments that have become familiar to every reasoner on this question. We only ask the right of deciding it for ourselves, and of being placed in this respect on an equal footing with other States. To the necessity of employing African laborers, which arises from climate, and the species of cultivation pursued in warm latitudes, is added a reason in this country peculiar to itself. The banks raised to restrain the waters of the Mississippi can only be kept in repair by those whose natural constitution and habits of labor enable them to resist the combined effects of a deleterious moisture, and a degree of heat intolerable to whites ; this labor is great, it requires many hands, and it is all important to the very existence of our country. If, therefore, this traffic is justifiable anywhere, it is surely in this province, where, unless it is permitted, cultivation must cease, the improvements of a century be destroyed, and the great river resume its empire over our ruined fields and demolished habitations. . . .

Deeply impressed, therefore, with a persuasion that our rights need only be stated to be recognized and allowed ; that the highest glory of a free nation is a communication of the blessings of freedom ; and that its best reputation is derived from a sacred regard to treaties . . .

We, therefore, respectfully pray that so much of the law above-mentioned, as provides for the temporary government of this country, as divides it into two Territories, and prohibits the importation of slaves, be repealed.

And that prompt and efficacious measures may be taken to incorporate the inhabitants of Louisiana into the Union of the United States, and admit them to all the rights, privileges, and immunities, of the citizens thereof.

Annals of Congress, 8 Cong., 2 sess. (Gales and Seaton, Washington, 1852), Appendix, 1597–1608 *passim*.

ENABLING ACT FOR LOUISIANA—1811

[ELEVENTH CONGRESS, THIRD SESSION]

An Act to enable the people of the Territory of Louisiana to form a constitution and state government, and for the admission of such state into the Union, on an equal footing with the original states, and for other purposes

Be it enacted by the Senate and House of Representatives of the United States of America in Congress assembled, That the inhabitants of all that part of the territory or country ceded under the name of Louisiana, by the treaty made at Paris on the thirtieth day of April, one thousand eight hundred and three, between the United States and France, contained within the following limits, that is to say: Beginning at the mouth of the river Sabine; thence by a line to be drawn along the middle of the said river, including all islands, to the thirty-second degree of latitude; thence due north to the northernmost part of the thirty-third degree of north latitude; thence along the said parallel of latitude to the river Mississippi; thence down the said river to the river Iberville; and from thence, along the middle of the said river and Lakes Maurepas and Ponchartrain, to the Gulf of Mexico; thence bounded by the said gulf to the place of beginning, including all islands within three leagues of the coast, be, and they are hereby, authorized to form for themselves a constitution and state government, and to assume such name as they may deem proper, under the provisions and upon the conditions hereinafter mentioned.

SEC. 2. *And be it further enacted,* That all free white male citizens of the United States, who shall have arrived at the age of twenty-one years, and resided within the said territory at least one year previous to the day of election, and shall have paid a territorial, county, or district, or parish tax, and all persons having in other respects the legal qualifications to vote for representatives in the general assembly of the said territory, be, and they are hereby, authorized to choose representatives to form a convention, who shall be apportioned amongst the several counties, districts, and parishes in the said territory of Orleans in such manner as the legislature of the said territory shall by law direct. The number of representatives shall not exceed sixty, and the elections for the representatives aforesaid shall take place on the third Monday in September next, and shall be conducted in the same manner as is now provided by the laws of the said territory for electing members for the house of representatives.

SEC. 3. *And be it further enacted,* That the members of the convention, when duly elected, be, and they are hereby, authorized to meet at the city of New Orleans, on the first Monday of November next, which convention, when met, shall first determine, by a majority of the whole number elected, whether it be expedient or not, at that time, to form a constitution and state government for the people within the said territory, and if it be determined to be expedient, then the convention shall in like manner declare, in behalf of the people of the said territory, that it adopts the constitution of the United States; whereupon the said convention shall be, and hereby is, authorized to form a constitution and state government for the people of the said territory: *Provided,* The constitution to be formed, in virtue of the authority herein given, shall be republican, and consistent with the constitution of the United States; that it shall contain the fundamental principles of civil and religious liberty; that it shall secure to

the citizen the trial by jury in all criminal cases, and the privilege of
the writ of *habeas corpus*, conformable to the provisions of the constitution of the United States; and that after the admission of the said
territory of Orleans as a state into the Union, the laws which such
state may pass shall be promulgated and its records of every description shall be preserved, and its judicial and legislative written proceedings conducted in the language in which the laws and the judicial
and legislative written proceedings of the United States are now
published and conducted: *And provided also,* That the said convention shall provide by an ordinance, irrevocable without the consent
of the United States, that the people inhabiting the said territory do
agree and declare that they forever disclaim all right or title to the
waste or unappropriated lands lying within the said territory, and
that the same shall be and remain at the sole and entire disposition
of the United States, and moreover that each and every tract of land
sold by Congress shall be and remain exempt from any tax laid by
the order or under the authority of the state, whether for state,
county, township, parish, or any other purpose whatever, for the
term of five years from and after the respective days of the sales
thereof, and that the lands belonging to citizens of the United States
residing without the said state shall never be taxed higher than the
lands belonging to persons residing therein, and that no taxes shall be
imposed on lands the property of the United States, and that the river
Mississippi and the navigable rivers and waters leading into the same
or into the Gulf of Mexico shall be common highways and forever
free, as well to the inhabitants of the said state as to other citizens
of the United States, without any tax, duty, impost, or toll therefor
imposed by the said state.

SEC. 4. *And be it further enacted,* That in case the convention shall
declare its assent in behalf of the people of the said territory to the
adoption of the constitution of the United States, and shall form a
constitution and state government for the people of the said territory
of Orleans, the said convention, as soon thereafter as may be, is hereby
required to cause to be transmitted to Congress the instrument by
which its assent to the constitution of the United States is thus given
and declared, and also a true and attested copy of such constitution or
frame of state government as shall be formed and provided by said
convention, and if the same shall not be disapproved by Congress, at
their next session after the receipt thereof, the said state shall be
admitted into the Union upon the same footing with the original
states.

SEC. 5. *And be it further enacted,* That five per centum of the net
proceeds of the sales of the lands of the United States, after the first
day of January, shall be applied to laying out and constructing
public roads and levees in the said state, as the legislature thereof may
direct.

Approved, February 20, 1811.

ACT FOR THE ADMISSION OF LOUISIANA—1812

[TWELFTH CONGRESS, FIRST SESSION]

An act for the admission of the state of Louisiana into the Union, and to extend the laws of the United States to the said state

Whereas the representatives of the people of all that part of the territory or country ceded, under the name of " Louisiana," by the treaty made at Paris on the thirtieth day of April, one thousand eight hundred and three, between the United States and France, contained within the following limits, that is to say: Beginning at the mouth of the river Sabine; thence, by a line to be drawn along the middle of said river, including all islands, to the thirty-second degree of latitude; thence due north to the northernmost part of the thirty-third degree of north latitude; thence along the said parallel of latitude to the river Mississippi: thence down the said river to the river Iberville; and from thence along the middle of the said river, and lakes Maurepas and Pontchartrain, to the gulf of Mexico; thence bounded by the said gulf to the place of beginning, including all islands within three leagues of the coast, did, on the twenty-second day of January, one thousand eight hundred and twelve, form for themselves a constitution and state government, and give to the said state the name of the state of Louisiana in pursuance of an act of Congress entitled "An act to enable the people of the territory of Orleans to form a constitution and state government, and for the admission of the said state into the Union on an equal footing with the original states, and for other purposes; " and the said constitution having been transmitted to Congress, and by them being hereby approved: Therefore,

Be it enacted by the Senate and House of Representatives of the United States of America, in Congress assembled, That the said state shall be one, and is hereby declared to be one, of the United States of America, and admitted into the Union on an equal footing with the original states, in all respects whatever, by the name and title of the state of Louisiana: *Provided,* That it shall be taken as a condition upon which the said state is incorporated in the Union, that the river Mississippi, and the navigable rivers and waters leading into the same, and into the gulf of Mexico, shall be common highways and forever free, as well to the inhabitants of the said state as to the inhabitants of other states and the territories of the United States, without any tax, duty, impost, or toll therefor, imposed by the said state; and that the above condition, and also all other the conditions and terms contained in the third section of the act, the title whereof is hereinbefore recited, shall be considered, deemed, and taken fundamental conditions and terms, upon which the said state is incorporated in the Union.

SEC. 2. *And be it further enacted,* That until the next general census and apportionment of representatives, the said state shall be entitled to one representative in the House of Representatives of the United States; and that all the laws of the United States not locally inapplicable shall be extended to the said state, and shall have the same force and effect within the same as elsewhere within the United States.

SEC. 3. *And be it further enacted*, That the said state. together with the residue of that portion of country which was comprehended within the territory of Orleans, as constituted by the act entituled "An act erecting Louisiana into two territories, and providing for the temporary government thereof," shall be one district, and be called the Louisiana district: and there shall be established in the said district a district court, to consist of one judge. who shall reside therein, and be called the district judge; and there shall be, annually, four stated sessions of the said court held at the city of Orleans: the first to commence on the third Monday in July next, and the three other sessions progressively, on the third Monday of every third calendar month thereafter. The said judge shall, in all things, have and exercise the same jurisdiction and powers which, by the act the title whereof is in this section recited, were given to the district judge of the territory of Orleans; and he shall be allowed an annual compensation of three thousand dollars. to be paid quarter-yearly at the treasury of the United States. The said judge shall appoint a clerk of the said court. who shall reside and keep the records of the court in the city of Orleans, and shall receive for the services performed by him the same fees heretofore allowed to the clerk of the Orleans territory.

SEC. 4. *And be it further enacted*, That there shall be appointed in the said district a person learned in the law, to act as attorney for the United States, who shall. in addition to his stated fees. be paid six hundred dollars annually as a full compensation for all extra services. There shall also be appointed a marshal for the said district, who shall perform the same duties, be subject to the same regulations and penalties, and be entitled to the same fees to which marshals in other districts are entitled for similar services; and shall, moreover, be paid two hundred dollars annually as a compensation for all extra services.

SEC. 5. *And be it further enacted*. That nothing in this act shall be construed to repeal the fourth section of an act entitled "An act for laying and collecting duties on imports and tonnage within the territories ceded to the United States by the treaty of the thirtieth of April, one thousand eight hundred and three, between the United States and the French Republic, and for other purposes;" and that the collection-district shall be and remain as thereby established.

SEC. 6. *And be it further enacted*, That this act shall commence and be in force from and after the thirtieth day of April, eighteen hundred and twelve.

Approved. April 8, 1812.

Campaign of New Orleans (1814–1815)

BY REVEREND GEORGE ROBERT GLEIG (1821)

Gleig began his military career as a subaltern under Wellington, and was then sent to America, where he took part in the campaigns against Washington, Baltimore, and New Orleans. At the end of the war he retired from the army and took orders. His account of the campaign in which he participated is considered the fairest of those written from the English side. — Bibliography: Winsor, *Narrative and Critical History*, VII, 420–427, 436–438; James Parton, *Andrew Jackson*, I, xvi–xvii; Channing and Hart, *Guide*, § 172.

. . . IT was evident that the longer an attack was delayed, the less likely was it to succeed ; that something must be done immediately every one perceived, but how to proceed, was the difficulty. If we attempted to storm the American lines, we should expose ourselves to almost certain destruction from their artillery ; to turn them, seemed to be impossible ; and to draw their troops by any manœuvring from behind their entrenchments, was a thing altogether out of the question. . . .

. . . It was determined to divide the army, to send part across the river, who should seize the enemy's guns, and turn them on themselves ; while the remainder should at the same time make a general assault along the whole entrenchment. . . .

. . . According to the preconcerted plan, Colonel Thornton's detachment was to cross the river immediately after dark. They were to push forward, so as to carry all the batteries, and point the guns before day light ; when, on the throwing up of a rocket, they were to commence firing upon the enemy's line, which at the same moment was to be attacked by the main of our army. . . .

. . . But, unfortunately, the loss of time nothing could repair. Instead of reaching the opposite bank, at latest by midnight, dawn was beginning to appear before the boats quitted the canal. . . . day had

Albert Bushnell Hart, ed. American History Told By Contemporaries. Vol. III. New York: The Macmillan Company, 1898.

parapet without ladders was impossible. Some few, indeed, by mount-
ing one upon another's shoulders, succeeded in entering the works, but
these were instantly overpowered, most of them killed, and the rest
taken ; while as many as stood without were exposed to a sweeping fire,
which cut them down by whole companies. It was in vain that the most
obstinate courage was displayed. They fell by the hands of men whom
they absolutely did not see ; for the Americans, without so much as lift-
ing their faces above the rampart, swung their firelocks by one arm over
the wall, and discharged them directly upon their heads. The whole
of the guns, likewise, from the opposite bank, kept up a well directed
and deadly cannonade upon their flank ; and thus were they destroyed
without an opportunity being given of displaying their valour, or obtaining so much as revenge.

Poor Pakenham saw how things were going, and did all that a General
could do to rally his broken troops. Riding towards the 44th which had
returned to the ground, but in great disorder, he called out for Colonel
Mullens to advance ; but that officer had disappeared, and was not to
be found. He, therefore, prepared to lead them on himself, and had
put himself at their head for that purpose, when he received a slight
wound in the knee from a musket ball, which killed his horse. Mount-
ing another, he again headed the 44th, when a second ball took effect
more fatally, and he dropped lifeless into the arms of his aide-de-camp.

Nor were Generals Gibbs and Keane inactive. Riding through the
ranks, they strove by all means to encourage the assailants and recall the
fugitives ; till at length both were wounded, and borne off the field. All
was now confusion and dismay. Without leaders, ignorant of what was
to be done, the troops first halted and then began to retire ; till finally
the retreat was changed into a flight, and they quitted the ground
in the utmost disorder. But the retreat was covered in gallant style
by the reserve. Making a forward motion, the 7th and 43d presented
the appearance of a renewed attack ; by which the enemy were so much
awed, that they did not venture beyond their lines in pursuit of the
fugitives.

While affairs were thus disastrously conducted in this quarter, the
party under Colonel Thornton had gained the landing place. On step-
ping a-shore, the first thing they beheld was a rocket thrown up as a
signal that the battle was begun. This unwelcome sight added wings to
their speed. Forming in one little column, and pushing forward a single
company as an advanced guard, they hastened on, and in half an hour

reached a canal, along the opposite brink of which a detachment of Americans was drawn up. To dislodge them was the work of a moment . . . This, however, was only an outpost. The main body was some way in rear, and amounted to no fewer than 1500 men.

It was not long, however, before they likewise presented themselves. Like their countrymen on the other side, they were strongly entrenched, a thick parapet with a ditch covering their front; while a battery upon their left swept the whole position, and two field pieces commanded the road. Of artillery, the assailants possessed not a single piece, nor any means, beyond what nature gave, of scaling the rampart. Yet nothing daunted by the obstacles before them, or by the immense odds to which they were opposed, dispositions for an immediate attack were made. . . .

. . . The sailors raising a shout, rushed forward, but were met by so heavy a discharge of grape and cannister, that for an instant they paused. Recovering themselves, however, they again pushed on; and the 85th dashing forward to their aid, they received a heavy fire of musketry, and endeavoured to charge. A smart firing was now for a few minutes kept up on both sides, but our people had no time to waste in distant fighting, and accordingly hurried on to storm the works; upon which, a panic seized the Americans, they lost their order, and fled, leaving us in possession of their tents, and of eighteen pieces of cannon. . . .

When in the act of storming these lines, the word was passed through our ranks, that all had gone well on the opposite bank. This naturally added to the vigour of the assault; but we had not followed our flying enemy above two miles, when we were commanded to halt. The real state of the case had now reached us, and the same messenger who brought the melancholy news, brought likewise an order to return. . . .

. . . General Lambert, on whom the chief command had devolved, very prudently determined not to risk the safety of his army by another attempt upon works evidently so much beyond their strength. He considered, and considered justly that his chances of success were in every respect lessened by the late repulse. . . . A retreat, therefore, while yet the measure appeared practicable, was resolved upon, and towards that end were all our future operations directed.

[George Robert Gleig.] *A Narrative of the Campaigns of the British Army at Washington and New Orleans* (London, 1821). 313-335 *passim*.

FREDERIKA BREMER'S DESCRIPTION OF NEW ORLEANS

This description of New Olreans, including its
beauties, the conditions of slavery and its prisons
is presented by this noted German literary figure.

Adolph B. Benson, ed. <u>America of the Fifties: Letters
of Frederika Bremer</u>. New York: The American-Scandinavian
Foundation, 1924.

New Orleans, Louisiana, Jan. 1, 1851. In one
of the slave houses I saw a gentleman whose ex-
terior and expression I shall never forget. He
seemed to be the owner of the slaves there, and
my companion requested permission for himself
and me to see them. He consented, but with an
air, and glance at me, as if he would annihilate
me. He was a man of unusual size, and singu-
larly handsome. His figure was Herculean, and
the head had the features of a Jupiter; but majesty
and gentleness were there converted into a hard-
ness which was really horrible. One might just as
well have talked about justice and humanity to a
block of stone as to that man. One could see by
the cold expression of that dark blue eye, by those
firmly-closed lips, that he had set his foot upon
his own conscience, made an end of all hesitation
and doubt, and bade defiance both to heaven and
hell. He *would* have *money.* If he could, by
crushing the whole human race in his hand, have
converted it into money, he would have done
so with pleasure. The whole world was to him
nothing excepting as a means of making money.
The whole world might go to rack and ruin so

that he could rise above it—a rich man, as the
only rich and powerful man in the world. If I
wanted to portray the image of perfected, hard-
ened selfishness, I would paint that beautiful head.
That perfectly dark expression of countenance—
the absence of light, life, joy—was only the more
striking because the complexion was fair; and the
cheeks, although somewhat sunken, had a beautiful bloom. He seemed to be about fifty.

On the 31st of December I went with my kind
and estimable physician to witness a slave-auction,
which took place not far from my abode. It was
held at one of the small auction-rooms which are
found in various parts of New Orleans. The principal scene of slave-auctions is a splendid rotunda,
the magnificent dome of which is worthy to re-
sound with songs of freedom. We entered a large
and somewhat cold and dirty hall on the basement
story of a house, where a great number of people
were assembled. About twenty gentlemanlike men
stood in a half circle around a dirty wooden platform, which for the moment was unoccupied. On
each side, by the wall, stood a number of black
men and women, silent and serious. The whole
assembly was silent, and it seemed to me as if a
heavy gray cloud rested upon it. One heard
through the open door the rain falling heavily in
the street. The gentlemen looked askance at me

with a gloomy expression, and probably wished
that they could send me to the North Pole.

Two gentlemen hastily entered; one of them,
a tall, stout man, with a gay and good-tempered
aspect, evidently a *bon vivant,* ascended the auction platform. I was told that he was an English-
man, and I can believe it from his blooming complexion, which was not American. He came
apparently from a good breakfast, and he seemed
to be actively employed in swallowing his last
mouthful. He took the auctioneer's hammer in
his hand, and addressed the assembly much as
follows: "The slaves which I now have to sell,
for what price I can get, are a few home-slaves,
all the property of one master. This gentleman
having given his bond for a friend who afterward
became bankrupt, has been obliged to meet his
responsibilities by parting with his faithful servants. These slaves are thus sold, not in consequence of any faults which they possess, or for any
deficiencies. They are all faithful and excellent
servants, and nothing but hard necessity would
have compelled their master to part with them.
They are worth the highest price, and he who
purchases them may be sure that he increases the
prosperity of his family."

After this he beckoned to a woman among the
blacks to come forward, and he gave her his hand

to mount upon the platform, where she remained standing beside him. She was a tall, well-grown mulatto, with a handsome but sorrowful countenance and a remarkably modest, noble demeanor. She bore on her arm a young sleeping child, upon which, during the whole auction ceremonial, she kept her eyes immovably riveted, with her head cast down. She wore a gray dress made to the throat, and a pale yellow handkerchief, checked with brown, was tied round her head. The auctioneer now began to laud this woman's good qualities, her skill and her abilities, to the assembly. He praised her character, her good disposition, order, fidelity; her uncommon qualifications for taking care of a house; her piety, her talents, and remarked that the child which she bore at her breast, and which was to be sold with her, also increased her value. After this he shouted with a loud voice, "Now, gentlemen, how much for this very superior woman, this remarkable, etc., etc., and her child?"

He pointed with his outstretched arm and forefinger from one to another of the gentlemen who stood around, and first one and then another replied to his appeal with a short silent nod, and all the while he continued in this style: "Do you offer me five hundred dollars? Gentlemen, I am offered five hundred dollars for this superior

woman and her child. It is a sum not to be thought
of! She, with her child, is worth double that
money. Five hundred and fifty, six hundred, six
hundred and fifty, six hundred and sixty, six
hundred and seventy. My good gentlemen, why
do you not at once say seven hundred dollars for
this uncommonly superior woman and her child?
Seven hundred dollars—it is downright robbery!
She would never have been sold at that price if
her master had not been so unfortunate," etc., etc.

The hammer fell heavily; the woman and her
child were sold for seven hundred dollars to one
of those dark, silent figures before her. Who he
was; whether he was good or bad; whether he
would lead her into tolerable or intolerable slavery
—of all this, the bought and sold woman and
mother knew as little as I did, neither to what part
of the world he would take her. And the father
of her child—where was he?

With eyes still riveted upon that sleeping child,
with dejected but yet submissive mien, the handsome mulatto stepped down from the auction-plat-
form to take her stand beside the wall, but on the
opposite side of the room. Next, a very dark
young negro girl stepped upon the platform. She
wore a bright yellow handkerchief tied very daint-
ily around her head, so that the two ends stood
out like little wings, one on each side. Her figure

was remarkably trim and neat, and her eyes glanced around the assembly both boldly and inquiringly. The auctioneer exalted her merits likewise, and then exclaimed, "How much for this very likely young girl?" She was soon sold, and, if I recollect rightly, for three hundred and fifty dollars.

After her a young man took his place on the platform. He was a mulatto, and had a remarkably good countenance, expressive of gentleness and refinement. He had been servant in his former master's family, had been brought up by him, was greatly beloved by him, and deserved to be so—a most excellent young man! He sold for six hundred dollars.

After this came an elderly woman, who had also one of those good-natured, excellent countenances so common among the black population, and whose demeanor and general appearance showed that she, too, had been in the service of a good master, and, having been accustomed to gentle treatment, had become gentle and happy. All these slaves, as well as the young girl, who looked pert rather than good, bore the impression of having been accustomed to an affectionate family life.

And now, what was to be their future fate? How bitterly, if they fell into the hands of the

wicked, would they feel the difference between
then and now—how horrible would be their lot!
The mother in particular, whose whole soul was
centered in her child, and who, perhaps, would
have soon to see that child sold away, far away
from her—what would then be her state of
mind! No sermon, no anti-slavery oration could
speak so powerfully against the institution of
slavery as this slave-auction itself! The master had been good, the servants good also, attached and faithful, and yet they were sold
to whoever would buy them—sold like brute
beasts!

Sunday, January 5. Yesterday forenoon I visited the prisons of the city, accompanied by the
superintendents and two distinguished lawyers.
The outward management cf the prisons seems
to me excellent. Order and cleanliness prevail
throughout, as is always the case wherever the
Anglo-American legislates. I noted some features of the internal management.

I visited some rooms where women accused of
capital offenses were confined. Their dress spoke
of circumstances far removed from poverty, but
their countenances of the prevalence of violent
and evil passions. Among them I remarked one
in particular, a lady charged with the murder of

her husband from jealousy, whose whole bearing denoted boldness and pride.

All these women declared their innocence and complained of injustice. Each one had her own apartment, but might avail herself of companionship in the piazza which surrounded the building within a court. There sat under this piazza a group of negro women, apparently enjoying the sun, which was then shining warmly. They looked so good and quiet, and they all, especially two young girls, bore so evidently the stamp of innocence and of good disposition, that I asked, with no small degree of astonishment:

"Why are these here? What crimes have they committed?"

"They have committed no offense whatever," was the reply. "But their master having given security for a person who is now bankrupt, they are brought in here to prevent their being seized and sold by auction to cover the demand; and here they will remain till their master finds an opportunity of recovering them."

"You see," said one of the lawyers, "that it is to defend them; it is for their advantage that they are here."

"How long will they probably remain here?" I inquired, cogitating within myself as to what particular advantage could be derived by the inno-

cent from that daily association with these white
ladies accused of the darkest crimes.

"Oh, at the most, two or three weeks—quite
a short time," replied the lawyer.

One of the negro girls smiled, half sadly, half
bitterly. "Two weeks!" said she; "we have
already been here two years!"

I looked at the lawyer. He seemed a little
confounded.

"Ah!" said he, "it is extraordinary; something
quite unusual—very unusual; altogether an excep-
tional case—very rare!" And he hurried away
from the place.

About January 27. I must now tell you about
a real African tornado which we witnessed last
Sunday afternoon. It was in the African Church,
for even here, in this gay, light-hearted city of
New Orleans, has Christianity commenced its
work of renovated life; and they have Sunday-
schools for negro children, where they receive
instruction about the Saviour; and the negro slaves
are able to serve God in their own church.

We came too late to hear the sermon in this
African Church, whither we had betaken ourselves. But at the close of the service a so-called
class-meeting was held. I do not know whether
I have already said that the Methodists form,

within their community, certain divisions or
classes, which elect their own leaders and exhorters. These exhorters go around at the class-meeting to such of the members of their class as they
deem to stand in need of consolation or encourage-
ment, talk to them, aloud or in an under voice,
receive their confessions, impart advice to them,
and so on. I had seen such a class-meeting at
Washington and knew therefore what was the
kind of scene which we might expect. But my
expectations were quite exceeded here. Here we
were nearer the tropical sun than at Washington.

The exhorters went round and began to con-
verse here and there with the people who sat on
the benches. Scarcely, however, had they talked
for a minute before the person addressed came
into a state of exaltation, and began to speak and
to perorate more loudly and more vehemently
than the exhorter himself, and so to overpower
him. There was one exhorter in particular, whose
black, good-natured countenance was illumined by
so great a degree of the inward light, by so much
good-humor and joy, that it was a pleasure to see
him, and to hear him, too; for, although his
phrases were pretty much the same, and the
same over again, yet they were words full of
Christian pith and marrow, and they were uttered
with so much cordiality, that they could not do

other than go straight to the heart with enlivening
power. Sometimes his ideas seemed to come to
an end, and he stood, as it were, seeking for a
moment; but then he would begin again with what
he had just now said, and his words always brought
with them the same warmth and faithfulness, and
he looked like a life-infusing sunbeam. And it
was only as the messenger of the joy in Christ
that he preached:

"Hold fast by Christ! He is the Lord! He
is the mighty One! He will help! He will do
everything well! Trust in Him, my sister, my
brother. Call upon Him. Yes. Yes. Hold
fast by Christ! He is the Lord!"

By degrees the noise increased in the church
and became a storm of voices and cries. The
words were heard, "Yes, come, Lord Jesus!
Come, oh come, oh glory!" and they who thus
cried aloud began to leap—leaped aloft with a
motion as of a cork flying out of a bottle, while
they waved their arms and their handkerchiefs
in the air, as if they were endeavoring to bring
something down, and all the while crying aloud,
"Come, oh come!" And as they leaped, they
twisted their bodies round in a sort of corkscrew
fashion, and were evidently in a state of convul-
sion; sometimes they fell down and rolled in the
aisle, amid loud, lamenting cries and groans. I

saw our tropical exhorter, the man with the sun-
bright countenance, talking to a young negro with
a crooked nose and eyes that squinted, and he too
very soon began to talk and to preach, as he sprang
high into the air, leaping up and down with in-
credible elasticity. Whichever way we looked
in the church, we saw somebody leaping up and
fanning the air; the whole church seemed trans-
formed into a regular bedlam, and the noise and
the tumult was horrible. Still, however, the exhorters made their rounds with beaming countenances, as if they were in their right element, and
as if everything were going on as it ought to do.
Presently we saw our hearty exhorter address a
few words to a tall, handsome mulatto woman,
who sat before us, and while he was preaching to
her she began to preach to him; both talked for
some time with evident pleasure, till she also
got into motion and sprang aloft with such vehe-
mence that three other women took hold of her
by the skirts, as if to hold her still on the earth.
Two of these laughed quietly, while they continued
to hold her down and she to leap up and throw
her arms around. At length she fell and rolled
about amid convulsive groans. After that she
rose up and began to walk about, up and down the
church, with outspread arms, ejaculating every
now and then, "Hallelujah!" Her appearance

was now calm, earnest, and really beautiful. Amid
all the wild tumult of crying and leaping, on the
right hand and the left, she continued to walk up
and down the church in all directions, with outspread arms, eyes cast upward, exclaiming in a low
voice, "Hallelujah! Hallelujah!" At length she
sank down upon her knees on the platform by the
altar, and there she became still.

After the crying and the leaping had continued
for a good quarter of an hour longer, several
negroes raised the mulatto woman, who was lying
prostrate by the altar. She was now quite rigid.
They bore her to a bench in front of us, and laid
her down upon it.

"What has happened to her?" we inquired
from a young negro girl whom she knew.

"Converted!" said she laconically, and joined
those who were softly rubbing the pulses of the
converted.

I laid my hand upon her brow. It was quite
cold; so, also, were her hands.

When, by degrees, she had recovered con-
sciousness, her glance was still fixed, but it seemed
to me that it was directed rather inwardly than
outwardly; she talked to herself in a low voice,
and such a beautiful, blissful expression was por-
trayed in her countenance that I would willingly
experience that which she then experienced, saw,

or perceived. It was no ordinary, no earthly
scene. Her countenance was, as it were, trans-
figured. As soon as she had returned to her usual
state, after deep sighs, her appearance became
normal also. But her demeanor was changed;
she wept much, but calmly and silently.

The tornado gradually subsided in the church;
shrieking and leaping, admonishing and preaching,
all became hushed; and now people shook hands
with each other, talked, laughed, congratulated
one another so heartily, so cheerfully, with such
cordial warmth and good will, that it was a pleasure to behold. Of the whole raging, exciting
scene there remained merely a feeling of satisfaction and pleasure, as if they had been together at
some joyful feast.

I confess, however, to having been thoroughly
amused by the frolic. Not so a friend, who re-
garded that disorderly, wild worship with a feeling of astonishment, almost of indignation; and
when our warm-hearted exhorter came up to us,
and, turning especially to her, apologized for not
having observed us before, that it was with no
intention to neglect us, and so on, I saw her lovely
coraled upper lip curl with a bitter scorn as she
replied, "I cannot see in what respect you have
neglected us." The man looked as if he would
have been glad, with all his heart, to have preached

to us, and, for my own part, I would gladly have
listened to his Christian exhortation, given with
its African ardor. We shook hands, however, in
the name of our common Lord and Master.

And spite of all the irrationality and want of
good taste which may be felt in such scenes, I am
certain that there is in them, although as yet in a
chaotic state, the element of true African worship. Give only intelligence, order, system to this
outbreak of the warm emotions, longings, and
presentiments of life, and then that which now
appears hideous will become beautiful, that which
is discordant will become harmonious. The children of Africa may yet give us a form of divine
worship in which invocation, supplication, and
songs of praise may respond to the inner life of
the fervent soul!

How many there are, even in our cold North,
who in their youthful years have felt an Africa
of religious life, and who might have produced
glorious flowers and fruits if it only could have
existed—if it had not been smothered by the snow
and the gray coldness of conventionality—had not
been imprisoned in the stone church of custom.

I have visited some other churches in New Orleans, a Unitarian, an Episcopalian, and a Catholic Church, the last with the name dear to me,
that of St. Theresa. But the heavenly spirit of

St. Theresa was not there.   An Irishman jabbered
an unintelligible jargon, and in not one of these
houses of God could I observe or obtain that which
I sought for—*edification*.   There was, at all events,
life and ardor in the church of the negro assembly.

(*To Her Majesty, Carolina Amalia, Queen
Dowager of Denmark*)

Cuba, West Indies, April, 1851.

Your Majesty—"Write to me from America!"
were Your Majesty's last kind words to me at parting, when I had the pleasure of seeing Your Majesty at Sorgenfri.

From Cuba, better than from any other point
on this side of the globe, I can speak of the New
World, because Cuba lies between North and
South America; the Anglo-Norman and the Spanish races here meet, for good and for evil, secretly
and openly combating for dominion; and in the
midst of this.wondrously beautiful scenery, which
belongs to the tropics (beneath which the greater
part of South America is situated), beneath the
tropical sun, among palm trees and coffee planta-
tions, one sees already the homes of the North
American, railroads, and shops.   The Anglo-
American "go-ahead" here comes in contact with

THE CAPTURE OF NEW ORLEANS

By Captain David G. Farragut

WITH characteristic modesty Captain, later Admiral, Farragut, reports to Gideon Welles, Secretary of the United States Navy, the capture of New Orleans by a Union squadron on April 27, 1862. His report, given here, was dated May 6, on board the flagship Hartford, anchored off New Orleans. Farragut, commanding a blockading fleet of 17 vessels, co-operated with a mortar flotilla of 25 vessels under Commander David G. Porter in running by Forts Jackson and St. Philip, which, facing each other across the Mississippi, guarded the approach to the city. The feat was accomplished under a terrific fire, in which Farragut's flagship, the Hartford, was badly damaged. With the loss of only one vessel, as here recounted, the Union fleet annihilated a Confederate flotilla of 13 gunboats and 2 ironclads. Immediately after Farragut took formal command of New Orleans, the city was occupied by Federal troops under General B. F. Butler.

SIR: I have the honor herewith to forward my report, in detail, of the battle of New Orleans. On the 23d of April I made all my arrangements for the attack on, and passage of, Forts Jackson and St. Philip.

Every vessel was as well prepared as the ingenuity of her commander and officers could suggest, both for the preservation of life and of the vessel, and perhaps there is not on record such a display of ingenuity as has been evinced in this little squadron. The first was by the engineer of the "Richmond," Mr. Moore, by suggesting that the sheet cables be stopped up and down on the sides in the line of the engines, which was immediately adopted by all the vessels.

America. Great Crises In Our History Told By Its Makers. Vol. 4. Chicago: Veterans of Foreign Wars Americanization Department, 1925.

Then each commander made his own arrangements
for stopping the shot from penetrating the boilers or
machinery, that might come in forward or abaft, by
hammocks, coal, bags of ashes, bags of sand, clothes-
bags, and, in fact, every device imaginable. The bul-
warks were lined with hammocks by some, with splin-
ter nettings made of ropes by others. Some rubbed
their vessels over with mud, to make their ships less
visible, and some whitewashed their decks, to make
things more visible by night during the fight, all of
which you will find mentioned in the reports of the
commanders. In the afternoon I visited each ship,
in order to know positively that each commander
understood my orders for the attack, and to see that
all was in readiness. I had looked to their efficiency
before. Every one appeared to understand his orders
well, and looked forward to the conflict with firm-
ness, but with anxiety, as it was to be in the night,
or at two o'clock A. M.

I had previously sent Captain Bell, with the petard
man, with Lieutenant Commanding Crosby, in the
"Pinola," and Lieutenant Commanding Caldwell, in
the "Itasca," to break the chain which crossed the
river and was supported by eight hulks, which were
strongly moored. This duty was not thoroughly performed, in consequence of the failure to ignite the
petards with the galvanic battery, and the great
strength of the current. Still it was a success, and,
under the circumstances, a highly meritorious one.

The vessel boarded by Lieutenant Commanding
Caldwell appears to have had her chains so secured
that they could be cast loose, which was done by that
officer, thereby making an opening sufficiently large
for the ships to pass through. It was all done under
a heavy fire and at a great hazard to the vessel, for
the particulars of which I refer you to Captain Bell's
report. Upon the night preceding the attack, however, I dispatched Lieutenant Commanding Caldwell
to make an examination, and to see that the passage
was still clear, and to make me a signal to that effect,
which he did at an early hour. The enemy commenced sending down fire-rafts and lighting their fires
on the shore opposite the chain about the same time,
which drew their fire on Lieutenant Commanding
Caldwell, but without injury. At about five minutes
of two o'clock A. M., April 24th, signal was made
to get under way (two ordinary red lights, so as not
to attract the attention of the enemy), but owing to
the great difficulty in purchasing their anchors, the
"Pensacola" and some of the other vessels were not
under way until half-past three. The enemy's lights,
while they discovered us to them, were, at the same
time, guides to us. We soon passed the barrier chains,
the right column taking Fort St. Philip, and the left
Fort Jackson. The fire became general, the smoke
dense, and we had nothing to aim at but the flash
of their guns; it was very difficult to distinguish
friends from foes. Captain Porter had, by arrange-
ment, moved up to a certain point on the Fort Jack-

son side with his gunboats, and I had assigned the
same post to Captain Swartwout, in the "Portsmouth," to engage the water batteries to the south-
ward and eastward of Fort Jackson, while his mortar
vessels poured a terrific fire of shells into it.   I discovered a fire-raft coming down upon us, and in at-
tempting to avoid it ran the ship on shore, and the ram
"Manassas," which I had not seen, lay on the opposite
side of it, and pushed it down upon us.   Our ship
was soon on fire half-way up to her tops, but we
backed off, and, through the good organization of our
fire department, and the great exertions of Captain
Wainwright and his first lieutenant, officers, and crew,
the fire was extinguished.   In the meantime our battery was never silent, but poured its missiles of death
into Fort St. Philip, opposite to which we had got by
this time, and it was silenced, with the exception of a
gun now and then.   By this time the enemy's gunboats, some thirteen in number, besides two iron-clad
rams, the "Manassas" and "Louisiana," had become
more visible.   We took them in hand, and, in the
course of a short time, destroyed eleven of them.   We
were now fairly past the forts, and the victory was
ours, but still here and there a gunboat made resist-
ance.   Two of them had attacked the "Varuna,"
which vessel, by her greater speed, was much in advance of us; they ran into her and caused her to sink,
but not before she had destroyed her adversaries, and
their wrecks now lie side by side, a monument to the
gallantry of Captain Boggs, his officers, and crew.   It

was a kind of guerilla; they were fighting in all directions. Captains Bailey and Bell, who were in command of the first and second divisions of gunboats, were as active in rendering assistance in every direction as lay in their power. Just as the scene appeared to be closing, the ram "Manassas" was seen coming up under full speed to attack us. I directed Captain Smith, in the "Mississippi," to turn and run her down; the order was instantly obeyed, by the "Mississippi" turning and going at her at full speed. Just as we expected to see the ram annihilated, when within fifty yards of each other, she put her helm hard aport, dodged the "Mississippi," and ran ashore. The "Mississippi" poured two broadsides into her, and sent her drifting down the river a total wreck. Thus closed our morning's fight.

The Department will perceive that after the organization and arrangements had been made, and we had fairly entered into the fight, the density of the smoke from guns and fire-rafts, and the scenes passing on board our own ship and around us (for it was as if the artillery of heaven were playing upon the earth), it was impossible for the Flag-Officer to see how each vessel was conducting itself, and can only judge by the final results and their special reports, which are herewith enclosed; but I feel that I can say with truth that it has rarely been the lot of a commander to be supported by officers of more indomitable courage or higher professional merit.

It now became me to look around for my little fleet,
and to my regret I found that three were missing—
the "Itasca," "Winona," and "Kennebec." Various
were the speculations as to their fate, whether they
had been sunk on the passage or had put back. I
therefore determined immediately to send Captain
Boggs, whose vessel was now sunk, through the
Quarantine bayou, around to Commander Porter,
telling him of our safe arrival, and to demand the surrender of the forts, and endeavor to get some tidings
of the missing vessels. I also sent a dispatch by him
to General Butler, informing him that the way was
clear for him to land his forces through the Quarantine bayou, in accordance with previous arrangements, and that I should leave gunboats there to protect him against the enemy, who, I now perceived, had
three or four gunboats left at the forts—the
"Louisiana," an iron-clad battery of sixteen guns; the
"McCrea," very similar in appearance to one of our
gunboats, and armed very much in the same way; the
"Defiance," and a river steamer transport.

We then proceeded up to New Orleans, leaving the
"Wissahickon" and "Kineo" to protect the landing of
the General's troops. Owing to the slowness of some
of the vessels, and our want of knowledge of the
river, we did not reach the English Turn until about
10:30 A. M. on the 25th; but all the morning I had
seen abundant evidence of the panic which had seized
the people in New Orleans. Cotton-loaded ships on
fire came floating down, and working implements of

every kind, such as are used in ship-yards. The destruction of property was awful. We soon descried the new earthwork forts on the old lines on both shores. We now formed and advanced in the same order, two lines, each line taking its respective work. Captain Bailey was still far in advance, not having noticed my signal for close order, which was to enable the slow vessels to come up. They opened on him a galling fire, which caused us to run up to his rescue; this gave them the advantage of a raking fire on us for upward of a mile with some twenty guns, while we had but two nine-inch guns on our forecastle to reply to them. It was not long, however, before we were enabled to bear away and give the forts a broadside of shells, shrapnel, and grape, the "Pensacola" at the same time passing up and giving a tremendous broadside of the same kind to the starboard fort; and, by the time we could reload, the "Brooklyn," Captain Craven, passed handsomely between us and the battery and delivered her broadside, and shut us out. By this time the other vessels had gotten up, and ranged in one after another, delivering their broadsides in spiteful revenge for their ill treatment of the little "Cayuga." The forts were silenced, and those who could run were running in every direction. We now passed up to the city and anchored immediately in front of it, and I sent Captain Bailey on shore to demand the surrender of it from the authorities, to which the Mayor replied that the city was under martial law, and that he had no authority. General

Lovell, who was present, stated that he should deliver up nothing, but in order to free the city from embarrassment he would restore the city authorities, and retire with his troops, which he did. The correspondence with the city authorities and myself is herewith annexed. I then seized all the steamboats and sent them down to Quarantine for General Butler's forces. Among the number of these boats is the famous "Tennessee," which our blockaders have been so long watching, but which, you will perceive, never get out.

The levee of New Orleans was one scene of desolation. Ships, steamers, cotton, coal, etc., were all in one common blaze, and our ingenuity was much taxed to avoid the floating conflagration.

I neglected to mention my having good information respecting the iron-clad rams which they were building. I sent Captain Lee up to seize the principal one, the "Mississippi," which was to be the terror of these seas, and no doubt would have been to a great extent; but she soon came floating by us all in flames, and passed down the river. Another was sunk immediately in front of the Custom-House; others were building in Algiers, just begun.

I next went above the city eight miles, to Carrollton, where I learned there were two other forts, but the panic had gone before me. I found the guns spiked, and the gun-carriages in flames. The first work, on the right, reaches from the Mississippi nearly over to Pontchartrain, and has twenty-nine guns; the one on the left had six guns, from which Commander Lee took some fifty barrels of powder, and completed the destruction of the gun-carriages, etc. A mile higher up there were two other earthworks, but not yet armed.

We discovered here, fastened to the right bank of the river, one of the most herculean labors I have ever seen—a raft and chain to extend across the river to prevent Foote's gunboats from descending. It is formed by placing three immense logs of not less than three or four feet in diameter and some thirty feet long; to the center one a two-inch chain is attached, running lengthwise the raft, and the three logs and chain are then frapped together by chains from one half to one inch, three or four layers, and there are ninety-six of these lengths composing the raft; it is at least three quarters of a mile long.

On the evening of the 29th Captain Bailey arrived from below with the gratifying intelligence that the forts had surrendered to Commander Porter, and had delivered up all public property, and were being paroled, and that the navy had been made to surrender unconditionally, as they had conducted themselves with bad faith, burning and sinking their vessels while a flag of truce was flying and the forts negotiating for their surrender, and the "Louisiana," their great iron-clad battery, blown up almost alongside of the vessel where they were negotiating; hence their officers were not paroled, but sent home to be treated according to the judgment of the Government.

General Butler came up the same day, and arrangements were made for bringing up his troops.

I sent on shore and hoisted the American flag on

the Custom-House, and hauled down the Louisiana
State flag from the City Hall, as the Mayor had
avowed that there was no man in New Orleans who
dared to haul it down; and my own convictions are
that if such an individual could have been found he
would have been assassinated.

Thus, sir, I have endeavored to give you an account
of my attack upon New Orleans, from our first move-
ment to the surrender of the city to General Butler,
whose troops are now in full occupation, protected,
however, by the "Pensacola," "Portsmouth," and one
gunboat, while I have sent a force of seven vessels,
under command of Captain Craven, up the river, to
keep up the panic as far as possible. The large ships,
I fear, will not be able to go higher than Baton Rouge,
while I have sent the smaller vessels, under Commander Lee, as high as Vicksburg, in the rear of
Jackson, to cut off their supplies from the West.

I trust, therefore, that it will be found by the Government that I have carried out my instructions to the
letter and to the best of my abilities, so far as this
city is concerned. All of which is respectfully submitted.

I am, sir, very respectfully, your obedient servant,

D. G. FARRAGUT.

Flag-Officer, Western Gulf Blockading Squadron.

Hon. Gideon Welles,
    Secretary of the Navy,
        Washington, D. C.

CLEANING UP A STATE

This description of the work of Louisiana in teaching its citizens about health and sanitation indicates how a mass program can be used to improve the health and living conditions of a large portion of the population.

Source: World's Work, March, 1912.

CLEANING UP A STATE

HOW DR. OSCAR DOWLING AND HIS HEALTH TRAIN MADE LOUISIANA SANITARY — A SERIOUS MAN WHO CHOSE A SPECTACULAR METHOD — SOME OF THE HUMORS OF SANITARY REFORM

BY

HENRY OYEN

I N AUGUST, 1910, when Dr. Oscar Dowling became president of the Louisiana State Board of Health, Louisiana was dirty, and didn't care. The every-day citizen didn't care how, where, or under what condition he secured his food supplies, and the average town didn't care if it dumped its sewage into the bayou that supplied its water.

To-day the citizens of this state are rapidly becoming enthusiasts on the subject of pure food. The towns are as jealous of the purity of their water supply as a Louisiana Tiger of his war record. In less than two years the people have been awakened from the insanitary slumber of decades and have become imbued with a spirit that promises to lift them from near the tail of the procession straight to a place among the leaders in sanitary civilization.

Dr. Dowling is the force that is responsible. Since his induction into office he has waged a campaign unique in the history of state officials in this country. "What's the matter with Louisiana?" "Dirt," was Dr. Dowling's verdict. And in two years he has forced a whole commonwealth literally to give itself a thorough washing.

To stand up before a state — especially one's own state — and tell it, not in carefully emasculated terms but in the short,

ugly words, that it is a dirty state and that its dirt is due wholly to dirty people, comes near to being an ultimate test of courage. But to do it in such a way that, though it shocked and awakened · the state as it seldom had been shocked or awakened before, it did not "make it mad," that surely must be considered a feat of genius — especially in proud, easy-going Louisiana.

Dr. Dowling said to his people: "We are all right, but we have got a bad reputation. Other states think of Louisiana as the home of swamps, and malaria, and mosquitoes, and fever, and general unhealthiness. We deserve this. It isn't true, but we deserve it. It's all our own fault. Our bad reputation is due not to climate, not to swamps, not to our geographical location, but to — dirt. Plain dirt. Dirt caused by dirtiness. Dirtiness accumulated through decades of carelessness. Dirt caused by dirty people. That's all that's the matter with us: we're a dirty crowd."

It didn't make much of an impression at first.

"Dirt?" said Louisiana "Of course there's some dirt. Always has been. Always will be. Folks are used to it. Everybody's got to eat a peck of dirt before he dies."

"No," said Dowling. "Cut the peck

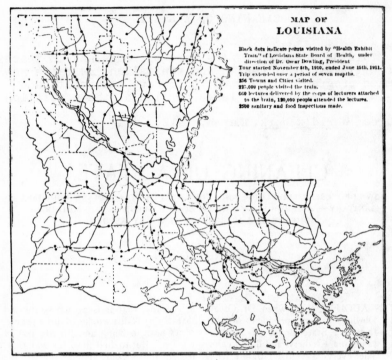

THE PATH OF THE HEALTH EXHIBIT TRAIN
WHICH WAS GIVEN TO DR. DOWLING BY THE RAILROADS, AND IN WHICH HE AND HIS STAFF LIVED FOR
SEVEN MONTHS

in half and you won't die half so soon and you'll live twice as much while you're living."

This was a new idea. It was a shock. Before the state had recovered, Dr. Dowling had his coat off and was up to his eyes in the work that he had shouldered: that of literally and physically giving a whole state a thorough cleaning. He is still at it, still "cutting the peck in half," and he is doing it in such a way that the state has learned to like it.

When Dr. Dowling became president of the state board of health in 1910 it was his first appearance in an official capacity. He had practised for fifteen years in Shreveport and had traveled much in the state. He knew what conditions were, and he knew that Louisiana, instead of preaching about its pleasant climate and fertile soil, must first of all wake up and have a sensational house-cleaning before it could hope to join the procession of progressive, prosperous states. He came to office with one firm conviction above all others: it was the duty of the health board's president to see that this house-cleaning was brought about.

The conditions that were to be faced were appalling. Louisiana was deep in the jungle of insanitation. There was little regulation of food or water supplies, or of physical conditions. Milk was produced by mangy, sickly herds in dairies where cleanliness never had been thought of. It was conveyed and sold to the consumer in a way that made purity impossible. Cattle were slaughtered under conditions that will not bear mention, and the meat was sold in markets where screens and scrubbing brushes were unthought of. Storekeepers kept their stocks of food with absolutely no thought of its condition. In a few stores in Louisiana flies and insects did not swarm in and out and over the exposed food supplies without hindrance. But they were so few as to be conspicuous.

In small towns the water supply was contaminated in terrible fashion. One third of the state has good water — supplied from artesian wells — but the remaining two thirds seemed to regard pure water as a minor matter. Children went to school in unimproved buildings. The common drinking cup, the public roller towel, habit-forming medicines, dirty streets, bad drainage, everything that breeds disease or communicates it, flourished in practially uncontrolled fashion.

To the People of Winnfield:

This is to notify you that I will discontinue my market after April 30th until I can meet the requirements of the State Board of Health, which will be only a short time.

I desire to thank my friends and customers for their past patronage and hope in the near future to be able to serve you again.

T. G. MILAM

A VISIBLE RESULT
OF THE EFFICIENCY OF DR. DOWLING'S MILITANT METHODS

To make the task of cleaning up more difficult, the easy-going Louisiana natives, lulled by the enviable combination of climate, magnolias, orange blossoms, and laughter of a land that care forgot, never had thought of seeing anything harmful in these conditions. never had stopped to connect them with a high death rate, much sickness, and a bad reputation. Things had been so ever since they could remember. Possibly they were deplorable. But the roses bloomed riotously in the front yard. The state was being kept back because of such things? Perhaps. But one got along fairly well in spite of it. A high death rate? Oh, well, people had got sick and died since the beginning of time.

These conditions and this spirit were not the exceptions but the rule.

Dowling knew that to alter this, to bring the state out of the jungle of insanitation to the light of civilization, ordinary methods would not suffice. A campaign of bulletins, publicity, and speeches wouldn't do it. A severe and shocking awakening must be effected. The gospel of health and cleanliness must be carried forth to the people and hammered home in a way that they could not forget.

The result was the Health Exhibit Train of the Louisiana State Board of Health, the celebrated "gospel of health on wheels."

"The people will not come to us to be shocked and awakened," said Dr. Dowling. "We will go to the people."

He talked the railroads into giving him two cars to carry cleanliness over unwashed Louisiana. The railroads laughed, humored him, and wound him up by making it three cars and by falling over themselves to take care of the train. Two of the cars were devoted to specimens, specimens calculated to shock the soundest sleeper, and dairy exhibits; the third was the living quarters of the health force.

"This car," said Dowling, "is to be our home until Louisiana has been washed."

It was. The health special left New Orleans November 5, 1910, a little more than two months after Dr. Dowling had come into office. Its tour ended June 5, 1911, seven months later. In this time it had covered 7,000 miles on the eight trunk lines within the state; had stopped in 256 cities and towns — every town in the state of more than 250 inhabitants; 660 lectures had been delivered to 120,000 people, 2,500 sanitary inspections had been made, and more than 225,000 visitors had passed through the cars and had health talked to them in a manner they would not forget. Every schoolhouse, jail, asylum, almshouse, practically every public institution in the state was visited and inspected. Most of the stores, restaurants, barber shops, hotels, butcher shops, slaughter houses, drug stores, dairies — every sort of business that might affect public health — went under the same inspection. Back yards, ponds, bayous, streets, barnyards, every odd corner where disease might lurk and breed and threaten a community, likewise. Where these things were found as they should be, compatible with good health — which was very, very seldom — Dowling said so. When they were found otherwise, which was very, very frequently, the doctor also said so. Markets, stores, restaurants, jails, almshouses were ordered closed or cleaned up, patent medicines were destroyed, tubercular beef burned. The doctor and his train and force of assistants went like a storm of cleanliness from one point in the state to the other, peering into dark corners, condemning, praising, teaching; and when it was over and the special was back in the yards in New Orleans, Louisiana was tingling from a new sensation: it had been washed.

One town after another went through the same mill that Dr. Dowling had planned. Upon the arrival of the train at a town, the time of which had been advertised to the local municipal, health, and school authorities, every member of the force hastened at once to fulfil his allotted duties. Dowling hurried to inspect the town's water and food supply, its public buildings, and sanitary conditions. He went everywhere. Sometimes he took a handcar and pumped his way down a narrow track, sometimes a motor car bore him into the country, sometimes a buggy, sometimes he walked. While he was thus occupied, the two physicians attached to the train were lecturing at the railroad stations and at public halls, and an instructor of School and Home Hygiene for the state — a woman — was talking to the children and women. In the evening a moving picture show, with films demonstrating the connection between dirt, flies, and disease, was given; and at the evening meetings Dr. Dowling told the assembled citizens how he had found things in their town.

" Thank God, our air and sunshine were reasonably good," said a Thibodeaux paper after the doctor's visit to that town. "Otherwise we wouldn't have a sanitary leg to stand on."

It was one shocked community after another — with rare exceptions — until the tour ended, and with the shock came the desired awakening. After putting in the day looking over a town, Dowling would stand up in the evening and say: "Today I inspected your town. John Jones's dairy is bad, Bill Smith's butcher shop is vile, Tom Johnson's restaurant is rotten. Your jail is impossible and your schoolhouse unfit to house children. I wouldn't care to shoulder the responsibility if an epidemic should break out here, which it is likely to do, if conditions remain as they are."

The Lake Charles *Press* said, after the tour had been in progress a few weeks, " Dr. Dowling has visited twenty parishes and inspected fifty-two towns, each of which he classified as ' bad,' ' worse,' or ' the limit,' as the case might be."

There were few towns that did not find some such classification. The Donaldsonville *Chief*, after the train's visit, said: " Donaldsonville got hers from the doctor. Dr. Dowling didn't quite denounce Donaldsonville as a desert of dirt. For the few oases, dear doc, many thanks. Well, the schoolhouse was clean, anyway."

As the tour progressed and the news of Dowling's denunciations became known, local papers began to carry such warnings: "The Health Train is coming on April 6th. This will give us plenty of time to clean up."

At one town the doctor upon his arrival said to the mayor: " Don't you want to clean up your town?"

"Why, doctor," was the reply, "we've been cleaning for a week."

The dirty condition of a public building was pointed out to its old time caretaker.

"Dr. Dowling, suh," said he, "your ideas on cleanliness, suh, differ from mine."

A baker in a small town was found at his dough with his hands and undershirt in hardly presentable condition.

"Hadn't you better wash up and change shirts?" suggested the doctor.

"Yessuh," said the man, proudly. "Tonight's the night."

Few men could have waged such a campaign against such conditions without incurring the enmity of the towns assailed. But Dowling damned them in a way to win their friendship.

" ..sery loves company. All the other dirty towns in the state will find satisfaction that the president of the state board of health roasted Baton Rouge as severely as he did any of us."

This was the spirit that began to manifest itself after the sting of the first shock had worn away.

The larger and older towns, the homes of Louisiana's aristocracy, were handled in the same brisk, ungloved fashion as the little mill towns up in the lumbering parishes. There was inevitable resentment here. But the new idea already had been accepted by the whole state. When a town grew indignant the other towns paused long enough in their labors of house cleaning to laugh at it, and presently the indignant one was turning to with pick, shovel, broom, and brush along with the rest.

Shreveport is Dr. Dowling's home town. He gave up a practice of $15,000 a year there when he accepted his present office at $5,000. Shreveport chortled as other towns writhed under the doctor's findings. Shreveport felt safe; the doctor wouldn't say anything harsh about his own town.

But he did. Shreveport went over the coals the same as the rest.

At a banquet given by the Shreveport Chamber of Commerce for the purpose of hearing the doctor tell them the things they didn't want to know, one tortured citizen was constrained to cry out. "Dr. Dowling, for God's sake, hush! I drink milk."

In another parish, one of the health force, upon being offered a drink of milk said: "Sir, I wouldn't drink anything but alcohol in this parish."

At Alexandria many school children at recess sought permission to go home.

"The doctors are coming," they explained, "and we want to get cleaned up."

An old colored mammy in a crowd awaiting the train broke out to her daughter; "Honey, you go home right quick and clean up that mess in yoh kitchen. Don't let them doctors think you ain't clean as yoh neighbors."

In one small town a woman conducted a country hotel. After Dr. Dowling's report on the place was read, the woman's little son threw his arms around his mother's neck and cried: "He says it will pass, mother, he says it will pass."

One hotel keeper, on being reprimanded for keeping a hog-pen just outside of his kitchen window, said: "Why doctor, those hogs have been there five months and

none of them ain't been sick yet."

A barber said to an inspector: "Ain't I a free citizen? Can't I be just about as dirty as I damn please?"

A butcher proudly displayed his tools. "Just cleaned 'em up, doctor."

Dowling promptly scraped half a pound of filth off one saw.

"Well, I didn't clean 'em that way," explained the man.

In one place the doctor remonstrated with a dairyman for currying his horse at the door of his milk room.

"Oh, that's all right, doctor," said he. "We get all that out when we strain the milk."

It was uphill fighting against such ignorance, but Dowling would not be denied.

"Clean up or shut up," he told dirty merchants and dairymen. One man, at least, shut up his business. The rest cleaned up.

In Madison Parish he condemned the almshouse as a relic of the dark ages unfit to house cattle in.

"I would rather have my life crushed out by slow torture," said he, "than have to stay in your almshouse. You remodel it and have it cleaned up or I'll have it torn down."

His orders were obeyed.

At one town he found the jail impossible.

"You clean that place up or you'll have to turn your prisoners loose. You can't keep such a filthy, disease-breeding place in this state."

The jail was cleaned up.

"There's no way of stopping that man," said an Alexandria citizen. "He's just bound to have his way."

He began to have his way after he had made it clear that he would have it in spite of good-natured opposition and carelessness. When this lesson had been firmly hammered home by a few choice examples, the towns began to fall in with the doctor's line of thinking.

In one town the mayor stepped forth and said: "This town was once the pride of the surrounding country and noted for its cleanliness but we've been in debt. Give us a few weeks and we'll show you that we know what a really clean town is."

Another place, Oakdale, had itself incorporated in order to acquire the authority to regulate conditions.

"First thing we know," said a country

editor, "we'll all be ashamed to be caught dirty."

Dowling had thoroughly awakened the state that had been dirty and didn't care.

The Health Exhibit Train was only one though the most important — of Dr. Dowling's efforts to bring good health to Louisiana. The abolition of public drinking cups and the public towel; the appointment of traveling salesmen as deputy health inspectors; the furnishing of anti-diphtheretic serum to the indigent; the regulation of barber shops, hotels, and restaurants; the registration and scoring of dairies; the regulation and control of fish and game, and the regulation of all food supplies; the screening of stores and markets; and the enthusiastic battles against the fly - all are achievements toward the same end.

By its new system of registering and scoring dairies, for instance, the State Board of Health makes it possible for every citizen who writes to it for the information to know under just what conditions the milk sold to his family is produced. Every citizen of the state is a potential health inspector. Every report of violations of the sanitary code is investigated by the board, and the transgressor warned and corrected. The citizens are beginning to make use of the board in the manner desired. Every day reports come to its offices in New Orleans concerning conditions in various towns, and inquiries concerning matters of health and sanitation.

In New Orleans, the Progressive Union stimulates the awakening by displaying on the curtains of moving picture shows such legends as:

"Do you know what the sanitary code is? Look it up. Maybe you are violating the law."

The health board expects that its work among the school children will bear the most valuable fruit. It is hard to start the adult native of an easy-going region along entirely different lines of thought and activity from those in which he has pleasantly lived, and lived as he wanted to all his life. But by putting the study of health into the public schools the next generations ... be inclined toward a different point of view. Every month the board of health sends a bulletin to every school child in the state. These

are placed in the hands of the school superintendents for direct distribution to the children. Teachers are constantly instructed in school and home hygiene, and they in turn communicate the knowledge to the children and their mothers. In Donaldsonville the first health parade that ever marched in the South was made by the children of the public schools.

It is a mistake to think of the man who is responsible for this as a story-telling "mixer," or as a man whose serious critical sense has been at all blunted by the development of his "mixing" talent. Dr. Dowling is first of all a grave, serious-minded physician. He romps with children, but he is very serious when talking about health. He has a genius for plunging to the centre of any problem, for taking hold of it and doing the essential thing without any waste effort. But he does not plunge until careful thought has showed him the way. He knew, as few knew, the serious need of awakening Louisiana to conditions in the state, and he knew the value of the spectacular. That is why he went at it as he did, not because his character loves the sensational. But his campaign was characteristic: he saw that the spectacular was the thing to do, and he did it.

He is a marvel in accomplishment. During the seven months that he was traveling on the health special, he averaged two talks a day, made his daily inspections, wrote his reports, and attended to his regular routine work as president of the State Health Board without hitch or confusion. At his office in New Orleans he performs feats at which the less strenuous natives gasp.

"Cicero," someone asked the doctor's office tender, "what time did the doctor get down this morning?"

"Dat Ah can't say, suh," said Cicero, "Ah didn't git down till foh thuhty mahself."

He has new ideas of how a state office should be run. He found it necessary to discharge a food inspector, and the man's friends and several of the papers howled. "I can't help it," said Dowling. "I am responsible for the efficiency of this office the same as if I was managing a business. I have got to have men who work for the interests of the public. Your man would not."

He is a big man physically, and nobody

has yet seen him tired. He tramps all day in the rain, inspecting dairies, and comes home ready to make a couple of red-hot speeches. He picks up children and rides them on his shoulder, then goes forth and damns their fathers for keeping dirty stores that may make children ill. He is one of the happiest men and one of the busiest. But he is serious about it all. His manner shows the kind of fight he has enlisted in. It is not a merry campaign of publicity. It is a stern, serious fight for civilization.

There was once a boy in a small country school whose general standing in the community was hampered by the unsavory reputation attached to him because of his dirtiness. One day a newly arrived teacher caught him, held him, and gave him a good scrubbing.

"Huh!" said the other boys. "He was just as clean as any of us, 'cepting for the dirt."

Dr. Oscar Dowling is the new teacher who has arrived in Louisiana.

BASIC FACTS

Capital: Baton Rouge.
Largest City: New Orleans.
Nicknames: Pelican State; Creole State.
Song: "Song of Louisiana."
Abbreviation: LA.

18th State to enter Union, April 30, 1812.
Area: 48,523 sq. mi.
Population (1970 Census): 3,652,000.

State Bird: Eastern Brown Pelican.

State Flower: Magnolia.

Congressional Districts of Louisiana

SELECTED BIBLIOGRAPHY

Arsenault, Bona. <u>History of Acadians</u>. Québec: Conseil de la vie francaise en Amérique, 1966.

Chambers, Henry Edward. <u>A History of Louisiana</u>. 3 vols. Chicago and New York: The American Historical Society, 1925.

Davis, Edwin Adams. <u>Louisiana, the Pelican State</u>, 3rd ed. Baton Rouge: Louisiana State University Press, 1969.

_____. <u>Story of Louisiana</u>. 4 vols. New Orleans: J. F. Hyer Publishing Co., 1960-63.

Dufour, Charles L. <u>Ten Flags in the Wind: Louisiana</u>. New York: Harper & Row, 1967.

Fortier, Alcée. A History of Louisiana. 4 vols. New York: Goupil & Co. of Paris, Manzi, Joy and Co., successors, 1904.

Gayarré, Charles. <u>History of Louisiana</u>. 4 vols. New Orleans: F. F. Harsell & bro., ltd., 1903.

Kallenbach, Joseph and Jessamine S. Kallenbach. <u>American State Governors, 1776-1976.</u> 3 vols. Dobbs Ferry, N. Y.: Oceana Publications, Inc., 1977-

Kane, Harnett Thomas. <u>Louisiana Hayride; The American Rehearsal for Dictatorship, 1928-1940</u>. New York: W. Morrow & Co., 1941.

King, Grace Elizabeth. <u>A History of Louisiana</u>. New Orleans: L. Graham Co., Ltd., 1905.

McGinty, Garnie William. <u>A History of Louisiana</u>. 3rd ed. New York: Exposition Press, 1951.

Robertson, James Alexander, ed. <u>Louisiana Under the Rule of Spain, France and the United States, 1785-1807</u>. 2 vols. Cleveland, Ohio: The Arthur H. Clark Co., 1911.

Sindler, Allan P. <u>Huey Long's Louisiana, State Politics, 1920-1952</u>. Baltimore: Johns Hopkins Press, 1956.

NAME INDEX